Spirits in My Bedroom

When the Bed is Too Crowded

Daylite Thompson

Spirits in My Bedroom
by
Daylite Thompson

Copyright © 2018 Daylite Thompson
All Rights Reserved.

All rights reserved. No part of this book may be reproduced or transmitted in any form or by any means, electronic or mechanical, including photocopying, recording, or by an information storage and retrieval system - except by a reviewer who may quote brief passages in a review to be printed in a magazine or newspaper - without permission in writing from the publisher.

ISBN-10: 978-0-578-84424-4

LCCN: 201901052

Cover Design by: Angel Bearfield

Edited by: So It Is Written, LLC
www.soitiswritten.net

Formatted by: Gloria Palmer Walker

Published by: Emperial Publishing

First Printing: November 2018
Second Printing: May 2020

Dedication

This book is dedicated to:
Pastor Christopher Joseph Whitsett (Papa)
October 19, 1964 - March 20, 2018
Thank you for your guidance.
I will carry on and make you proud.
Rest well. I love you.

୨⭒୧

To my brother and sisters:
Navada, Charlie (Tiffany), Raynard, Roger (LaShanda) and Dalerecia,
You can't get rid of me.
You all are stuck with me for life.
You all support me, no matter how crazy my dreams may seem. I'll always love you.
Our love can never be replaced.
I hope you all are proud of me.
Love you all, infinity times infinity.

୨⭒୧

To my spiritual mother, Mama Mary:
You have loved me like your own daughter.
You have been there to love me and scold me.
But, in it all, you have imparted wisdom in me,
not in just what you say, but in how you live.
Thank you for all you do.
I love you.

Acknowledgements

Thank you to my Lord and Savior for the ability to write and articulate the difficult situations of my life. Lord, I thank you for every negative situation you have allowed me to live through. Thank you for the ability to tell just a portion of my story in hopes that someone will learn what true forgiveness is.

A special thank you to Tonja "The Shoe Lady" Ayers, who inspired me and encouraged me to become an author. When we sat in your den, watching *Spirits In My Bedroom,* the stage production, you said, "I have one question: Where is the book?" The conversation we had after that question motivated me to become an author. It took what seemed to be years, but I finished it. I thank you.

Thank you, Courtney Whitty. You've been with me from day one, when all I had was a vision. You helped me bring my first stage production to life and have been encouraging me ever since. I've watched you grow into a beautiful woman, "The Diva." But remember, I am always big sister. Love you to life, Court. We still are going to get our big office.

Pastor Christopher Whitsett (Papa): Thank you for the time you took to read the book. I know you drove a long way just to spend a few hours with me. There are some things you can't pay a person for, and friendship is one of those things. Thank you for your friendship. Over the years, you and Kim have been such an inspiration in my life. We may not talk every day, but I've got your back, and I know you and Kim have mine. Love you both beyond life. Your input was priceless.

To my sister, LaShanda Davis: You are such an encourager. Thank you for believing in me and my dreams; your input was valuable. I knew when I chose you for the reading, you would be able to separate sisterhood and tell me if this was some garbage. That's why you had to be a part of the reading.

Auntie Shirley: You were the first to read the first rough draft. When you said you liked it, I was so excited. You told me to clarify a few parts, and I went back and did just that. I hope you enjoy the final copy.

To my best friend, Alisha Turner: We cry together, laugh together and dream together. Thank you for *repeatedly* telling me, "Get it done!" Your friendship means so much to me.

Melissa Talbot: You are such an asset to everything you touch. I wish I could keep you all to myself, but the talent you possess could never be wasted on just one person. I thank God for meeting you.

To my son, Keith Wright (my Navy guy): Thank you for sharing your ideas, words of wisdom and encouragement. You could have chosen to be anything in life, and you chose to be a son that a mother can be proud of. I thank you for being "one" of three of the best sons I have.

To Tyrone Wright (my 4.0 college graduate) and Sheldon Boyer (my Marine): Your mama did it, and I hope you all are proud. All of you are the *greatest* sons a mother could ask for.

To all my family: Thank you for your support.

To my mother, Dorothy L. Boyer and my father, Charles P. Boyer: Although you aren't here to see your baby publish her first book, I know you both would have been proud. You're always in my heart. Love you still and forever.

Again, thank you, God, for the ability to forgive.

Daylite

Spirits in My Bedroom

Introduction

From a young age, black boys are taught to be protectors. They are taught to protect their mothers, sisters, and family in general. When the father isn't around, many boys are the man of the house. I've always heard older men tell us younger boys, "The worst thing you can do is grow up to be a weak man. Real men work, real men provide, and real men don't cry." I believe teaching a young boy that, "Real mean don't cry" causes him to grow up with an erroneous misconception of life because, here I stand as a grown man, wondering when I get my chance to cry.

As a boy, people told me, "You need to be a man, boy." I never understood what that meant. I often sat in silence, wondering, *How do I be a man? How do men handle things? Outside of physical features, what does a man look like? How does a man talk? What does a man smell like? How does a man walk? Does he give a firm handshake? Or does he give a firm handshake only to that man who appears to be weaker than he is?* More than anything, the biggest question I stand here today and ask myself is, "How do I teach my son how to be a man, when I struggle with my own inconsistencies of being a man?"

I am twenty-six years old, and I'm still searching for someone to teach me what a man is. Since the age of twelve, I've struggled with trying to understand how the things I learned from my mother completely contradict the evil things I've seen as a boy.

Society has deemed me a man because I was born a boy. Once you become a certain age, the world doesn't care what you did or did not learn in your childhood. They simply look at you as a grown man. I attempt to function as a man every day, but I'm simply mimicking what I saw my best friend Gavin's father accomplish as a man. Gavin's father was my only example of what a man was supposed to look like. But, even in that, I still didn't know what attributes to look for in a man after the man who was supposed to instruct me and teach me abandoned me. This did nothing but confuse me.

My mother taught me all about life, but she never prepared me for the vicissitudes that were sure to come my way. Growing up, it looked like men had all the answers. Mothers worldwide used to tell their children, "Go ask your father." The man always worked. The man always got the big piece of chicken at dinner. So, I grew up thinking that men have all the answers, and I made sure I became a know-it-all.

I finished high school, graduated college, and I worked hard. I've made a good life for myself and I take care of my family. However, my mind is trapped at the age of twelve. I am a damaged little boy inside a man's body that's still sitting in his bedroom, hurting. In society's eyes, once you become a man, you just need to figure it all out on your own. That leaves most grown men empty, searching for what they should have received when they were growing up.

I guess the statement, "It takes men longer to grow up" is somewhat true. Now I am a grown man, who lacks direction, love and self-respect. I have truly lost my way. I have so many undisclosed secrets, hurts and pains. My life is full of indiscretions. I am the master of idiocy and I'm trapped by the perversions of my mind. However, I hide behind the successes of my life because I don't know how to confront this misrepresentation of a man who people see. I hate my falsified life. I'm a grown man who needs to cry, but I can't because I'm bound by the *spirits in my bedroom*.

Chapter 1
Birthday Celebration

It was my big day: my birthday. I turned twelve years old. Normally, my mother would have to call me three or four times before I got up to get ready for school. But on this day, I was so excited that I woke up before my alarm went off. By the time my mother called me, I was already dressed for school.

I ran downstairs to the kitchen, waiting for my mom and little sister Mya to yell, "Happy birthday!" However, my mom was rushing to get Mya off to school so she wouldn't be late for work. They both forgot to say, "Happy birthday!" This was strange because my mom never forgot our birthdays. So, I expected a big surprise when I got home from school.

Since my school wasn't far, and I had to be at school later than my sister, my mother usually left breakfast on the table for me while she took Mya to school. But, before we all left the house every day, my mother brought us into the living room and prayed for our protection and our safe return home. She also prayed that we had a good day. Mom would kiss me on the forehead. I would give Mya a great big hug, eat my breakfast, and leave for school shortly after my mom and Mya left.

Because it was my birthday, my teacher, Mrs. Rain, was bringing cupcakes for the whole class. The whole class was going to sing to me. I couldn't wait. I was one of the best students in the class, and I got teased a lot because I was known as the teacher's pet. I loved my teachers and they loved me. I was determined to be the best at whatever I was going to be. If I was going to drive an ice cream truck, I was going to be the owner of the ice cream brand sold on the truck. My mother made us feel like nothing was impossible. She always told us to reach for the stars and not to accept anything less than all of them.

When I got to school, all my classmates knew it was my birthday. I wore a birthday hat that I'd made so that, even while I was walking down the hallway, everyone who didn't know it was my birthday wished me a happy birthday because they saw my hat. Nothing could ruin my day. I'd been looking forward to my twelfth birthday for months. Furthermore, I was looking forward to the surprise my mother was going to have for me when I got home.

At lunchtime, my teacher got everyone's attention. They sang *Happy Birthday* and shared the cupcakes Mrs. Rain had brought in. Of course, the day was all about me. So, Mrs. Rain said I didn't have to take the pop quiz she was giving that day. I got straight A's in her class, so I probably would have aced the test anyway. The other students didn't get mad because I gave them the answers behind Mrs. Rain's back.

We were down to the last twenty minutes of class and I couldn't wait to get home. I sat in class, squirming, waiting for the last bell to ring. At some point, it looked as if the clock had stopped moving. I anxiously awaited the clock to strike 3:05 p.m. *Ring!* When the bell rang, I had to be the first person to run out the school.

It was such a beautiful day. The sun was shining, and the sky was clear. The birds were flying and chirping, and the air smelled of early summer barbeque. People were riding their bikes, driving their fancy cars with their windows and drop-tops down, and music blaring. A hint of the summer to come was in the air.

I had no clue what to expect, but something was strange when I got to my block. It seemed unusually quiet. It was peculiar that no one was outside on their porch. No one was watering their grass or washing their cars. This was bizarre because there was always someone outside on my block. The older people on our block always looked out for the kids in the neighborhood, except for today. I didn't let it bother me, though, because I was excited about getting home for my birthday surprise.

I ran down my block as fast as I could. I got to my front door, used my key to turn the lock, and when I opened the door, I had the biggest smile on my face. I was waiting for the yells and screams of, "Surprise!" But there was nothing—no decorations and no surprise. The house was just as clean as it was when we all left that morning.

I ran through the house, calling for my mom and Mya. I yelled, "Anyone home?"

I ran upstairs to my mother's room; she wasn't there. I went into Mya's room and she wasn't there either. I thought, *Something must be wrong*. My mother worked the early shift so she could take Mya to school and pick her up, but she was always home before me.

I walked back down the stairs, opened the front door, and stood on the porch. I looked up and down the street, and I still didn't see anyone outside. While I was running up the block in excitement, I hadn't even noticed my mother's car wasn't in the driveway. I came back in the house. Now I was seriously worried about my mother and Mya.

I walked into the kitchen and picked up the phone. As I was dialing my mom's cell number, I saw something moving through the sheer panels that covered the glass patio door. The patio door led to the backyard. So, I slowly walked to the door because I saw a string hanging from the glass. When I pulled the curtain back, I saw big gold numbers one and two. I opened the patio door and heard a loud boom. Sparkles came out the corners of the door followed by a loud, "Surprise!"

The surprise scared me so badly that I dropped the phone and peed my pants. I slammed the patio door before anyone could see that I peed my pants and I ran as fast as I could to my bedroom. My mom thought I was just scared, so she came running after me. I hid in my bedroom and told my mom I would be out in a moment. I didn't want anyone to know I wet my pants. I cleaned myself up as fast as I could and ran back downstairs. This time when I opened the patio door, I was ready for the biggest surprise birthday party ever. Since no one knew I wet my pants, when I opened the patio door again, I had the biggest smile on my face. Everyone said, "Surprise!" all over again.

My mother had outdone herself, as she did every year. There were gold balloons with the number twelve all around the backyard. I had twelve of everything: twelve gifts on the table, twelve different pizzas, and even twelve different flavors of Kool-Aid, which was my favorite drink.

I was surprised that my grandparents had flown all the way from Chicago just to bring me a gift. My best friend Gavin was there, along with some of my cousins and Mya. Now I knew why no one was outside when I got home from school. Everyone was hiding out in my backyard! My mom hired a DJ, who played all the popular songs from the radio. It was four hours of laughing, singing, dancing and eating. My twelfth birthday party was the greatest day of my life.

When my party ended, Grandma and Grandpa had to hurry to catch their plane back to Chicago. Mom wanted them to stay the night and leave in the morning, but Grandma said they had tickets for the same day. It would cost too much to change them and they didn't come prepared to stay. Grandma had airport service pick them up to take them back to the airport. But, before they left, in good ol' Grandma fashion, she gave me the biggest kiss a grandmother could give a birthday boy.

Grandpa was always the coolest guy I knew. We even had a special handshake we did: two up, two down, two to the left, never make it to the right, turn around twice, and make it nice! Boom! We both laughed every time we did it. Grandpa kissed my forehead and said, "Happy birthday, champ." I love my grandparents. Even though I hated it when they retired and moved to Chicago, they were living in their dream home and they were happy.

My party was named the party of the year. I knew people would talk about it for months to come. Once everyone was gone, I was still the happiest little boy in the world. I offered to help my mother clean up, but she told me Mya would help her. She told me to take my gifts to my room, get my bath and get ready for bed. I always did what my mother told me, so I did just that.

I entered my bedroom singing, "Happy birthday to me," still basking in the excitement from my birthday party. As I was putting away my gifts, I heard footsteps coming up the stairs. My bedroom door slowly cracked open. I knew my good day was coming to an end. His deep, heavy voice came through the crack in the doorway as he dragged out my name when he called me.

"Kyyy-llle."

The way he called my name always creeped me out. I turned around and glanced up at him as he entered my bedroom. He stood there, looking as if he had just left one of his business meetings. He was dark-skinned, about five-eight and huskily built. He had small, beady eyes, a big nose, and medium-sized lips. He wore black pants with a white button-up shirt, a gray suit jacket, a black and grey necktie and black shoes. He also had a cigarette hanging from his mouth. Ronald was my stepfather.

I never liked him, and he never liked me. Ronald is Mya's father and he made sure he treated us differently. Mya got away with everything, but he sure didn't believe in sparing the rod on me. He made sure I was chastised for anything and everything I did—or he *thought* I would do. He always said my mother did too much for me. So, every chance he got, he was going to teach me how *not* to be a mama's boy.

He came in my bedroom, closed the door, and said, "Kyle, I'm sorry I couldn't make it to your little birthday party." He took the cigarette from his mouth and put the fire out with his fingertips.

I hated this man so much that I used to hope his fingers would catch on fire. Since he wasn't my real father, I didn't care that he wasn't at my birthday party.

I responded, "Ronald, it's okay. I had a wonderful time without you. My mother told me to go to bed, so I'm getting ready for bed now."

He broke out in such a disdainful laugh that I didn't know what to expect. Usually, if he was going to beat me, my mother and my sister weren't home. This is how he got away with it. Whenever Ronald entered the room, my knees shook. I never spoke a word about the abuse to anyone. Ronald told me I'd, "better forever keep my mouth shut." Because I was so scared of him, I never said a word. My mother was so happily in love with Ronald that I didn't want to be the one to destroy her happiness. When Ronald abused me, I tried to think happy thoughts. I made my mind go as far away from my bedroom as I could. But I couldn't escape his horrible laugh or his presence, which darkened the room whenever he walked in.

He said, "I have a gift for you."

I didn't want anything from him. I called this man The Spawn of Satan. The previous year on my birthday, his gift was eleven lashes with his belt on the front lawn in front of all my friends. As funny as my friends thought it was, I was humiliated. Gavin was my only friend who didn't think it was funny. My mother stopped him once she heard all the commotion and they argued that night. That was the first time I saw him hit my mother. Mya and I heard them fight frequently since that day, which made me hate Ronald even more.

My biological father left my mother when I was just three months old, and no one has heard from him since. Everyone thought I hated Ronald because he wasn't my biological father. I hated Ronald because Ronald *hated me* and, by my standards, he treated my mother awful. But my mother was in love.

Ronald began to take his belt off. I immediately ran to the edge of my bed and fell on my knees. My mother taught me how to pray years ago. When the abuse from Ronald started, I changed the words of the prayer she taught me and simply prayed, "Now I lay me down to sleep. I pray, my Lord, my soul to keep. I'm on my knees, just like you said. Lord, please remove these *spirits from my bed.*" I repeated my prayer, hoping God's angels would show up just like in the movies and stop the bad guy from hurting the good person.

As I kept praying, I felt Ronald grab me from behind as he yelled at me, saying how ungrateful I was and how he was going to show me how not to be a mama's boy.

He yelled at me, "Shut up because real men don't cry!"

Immediately, I thought, *But I'm a little boy, and we do cry. I just don't want you to hurt me anymore.*

I never spoke a word to my mother about his abuse, but my mother was home this night. I was hoping she would hear him, come into my room, and make him stop. He told me repeatedly that this would teach me how to be a man. If this was teaching me how to become a man, I never wanted to be a man. This was when my fear of becoming a man set in. I never wanted to grow up because I knew that all the feelings of hatred and anger I harbored in my heart and mind would not make for a good man.

That night, knowing my mother was home, I decided to fight him back. I hoped I could cause such a commotion that my mother would come running and catch him in the act. I was tired of being abused. As I repeated my prayers, for the first time, I felt like God had sent my angel to rescue me from this awful demon. My mother came barging through the door.

I thought, *Finally! She caught him! Now she will understand why I hate this man so much.*

I heard her yell from across the room, "Ronald! Wha—"

If she said anything else, I didn't hear it. I saw my mother jump on the bed and leap on Ronald's back. She punched him as hard as she could. Ronald and my mother had fought many times before, but I had never seen my mother fight him like this. My mother wasn't a small woman. She stood five feet, eight inches tall, weighed one hundred and eighty pounds, and was solid. Her attack on Ronald was so unexpected that it took him a moment to get control of himself. My mother was going crazy on him. But then, Ronald started overpowering my mother.

Mya came running into the room, trying to figure out what was going on. I grabbed Mya to console her.

She yelled, "Daddy! Daddy! Please stop! Please stop!"

Mya tried to get between them as she hit Ronald, yelling for him to stop. Ronald yelled at Mya to move, which frightened her even more. She ran back to me, crying. This was the only time I wished I was already a man because I would grab Ronald and beat him until he would have stopped breathing. As I was trying to calm Mya down, I saw Ronald grab my mother and throw her against the wall. My mother immediately grabbed her chest. Mya was still yelling and crying.

Ronald turned to me and yelled, "This is all your fault!"

Just before he could grab me again, Mya screamed frantically, "Daddy, there's something wrong with Mommy!"

Ronald turned and looked at my mom. It was as if he was paralyzed for the moment. He slowly stumbled to my mother, calling her name, as Mya stood next to me and we looked on. When Ronald reached my mother, he yelled, "Someone call 9-1-1!"

Ronald continued talking to my mother, telling her to breathe. "You're going to be alright. Baby, I'm sorry."

I ran to the phone and dialed 9-1-1. I gave our address and my name. I told them, "Hurry! It looks like my mother can't breathe."

The operator told me, "Stay on the line with me."

Meanwhile, Ronald kept saying, "Breathe, baby! Breathe, baby! I need you to breathe!"

Mya and I were petrified, but it didn't take long for the emergency personnel to get to our house. I yelled to the operator, "They're here!" Then, I dropped the phone and ran as fast as I could down the stairs to open the door and let them in. I told them, "It's my mom! She's upstairs in my bedroom!"

The police, firefighters, and both a male and female paramedic arrived. I ran back up the stairs to show them where my mother was. They immediately went to work on her. The police officer saw that Mya and I were upset, so she asked us to come downstairs with her. Mya and I sat on the sofa.

The policewoman asked, "Is there an adult you could call to come get you all?"

I said, "Yes, but why? Why can't we go to the hospital with our mother?"

Mya hit me and whispered, "You know we aren't supposed to question adults."

Just as Mya said that, I saw Mrs. Washington coming across the street. Mya ran to Mrs. Washington and said, "Something's wrong with Mommy."

The policewoman asked, "Would it be okay if you all went to her house until we get your mother stabilized?"

Mrs. Washington said, "Of course, they can come with me. We're like family."

We went across the street… and waited and waited. Mrs. Washington tried to keep our spirits up, but she was just as worried about my mother as we were. My mom and Mrs. Washington had been friends since high school. That's how her son Gavin became my best friend when we grew up together, even though I was older than Gavin. It seemed like we waited for hours for someone to come tell us something.

Finally, there was a knock at the door.

Mr. Washington opened the door. Ronald just stood there until Mr. Washington invited him in. He entered and I couldn't wait. I ran up to Ronald, but before I could speak, I saw this look in his eyes. So, I backed up. I thought he was going to start beating me right in front of Mr. and Mrs. Washington. Ronald looked at Mr. and Mrs. Washington, then he looked over at Mya. There was a long pause.

I couldn't hold it any longer. "Well?"

Ronald's head slumped between his shoulders and he said, "Kyle and Mya, your mother is dead."

Chapter 2
Kyle

After my mother died, I wanted so badly to find my biological father. But I didn't have any information on him, so my search was over before it ever began. My twelfth birthday was supposed to be the best day of my life; instead, it turned out to be the worst day of my life.

My mother's cause of death was ruled a heart attack; however, the secret to the real cause of her death remains trapped in my bedroom. I wish I hadn't been too scared to speak up and tell the police. It surely would have changed my mother's cause of death from a heart attack to manslaughter, and that surely would have sent Ronald to jail. But the tears Mya cried, and the pain from both of our broken hearts, convinced me not to come forth and tell my side of what truly had happened in my bedroom. So, I buried the abuse, the pain and the lies, along with the fabricated story Ronald gave to the police about entering in the room and finding my mom having a heart attack.

My mother came into that room, did everything she could to protect me, and lost her life because of it. I found it difficult to live after the loss of my mother. I often wondered who I was going to look to for strength, guidance and answers now that she was gone. I became completely lost without her. God took my mother away from me on my twelfth birthday.

And on that day, I vowed I would never serve, praise or love God again.

After everything Ronald had done to me, plus knowing he was responsible for my mother's death, I hated him more than words. I loathed him. I despised him and everything he stood for. This hatred grew deeper inside me by the minute. I was twelve years old, confused and alone. I hated the world and everything in it, except my baby sister, Mya.

It was difficult for us to make it through the days, the hours and the minutes that followed my mom's death. The pain, at times, was unbearable and too hard to discuss. So, most of the time, we agreed not to talk about it at all. Mya wasn't sure what had really happened in my bedroom, and I couldn't tell her the whole story. I thought I would be able to put the events of my mother's death behind me and move on. Instead, I became a prisoner of her death *and my bedroom*.

Ronald and my mother had a large insurance policy, so he spared no expense for her homegoing. My mother had top-of-the-line everything. I believe he spent so much on her homegoing out of the guilt he felt for killing her.

Grandma and Grandpa came to stay with us for a few weeks, just to help us out. We were at the end of the school year, with only about two weeks left. So, we didn't return to school. Our teachers were understanding, and we were already honor-roll students. So, missing the rest of the school year didn't affect us. We still passed with honors.

After a few weeks, the phones stopped ringing. People stopped checking on us. Grandma and Grandpa went back home, and real life with Ronald as our sole guardian began. I was so angry and bitter; I knew I would never forgive Ronald for what he had done to my mother, my sister and me. I sometimes prayed that Ronald would just lie down and die. I knew that feeling didn't resemble anything my mother had taught me. The guilt he carried from my mother's death slowly started to destroy him from the inside out, right before our eyes.

For months, I slept in Mya's room on the floor next to her bed because, every time I went into my bedroom, I relived the night my mother died. I couldn't handle it. Sometimes, I woke up and Mya would be lying on the floor right next to me. Most nights, I wouldn't go to sleep until Mya was sleep. Other nights, she would wake me up in the middle of the night, crying. I cried with her and held her as we cried ourselves to sleep.

My mother wasn't a drinker, but Ronald was. Mya and I both noticed that Ronald started drinking more. We had a bar in our home, and it stayed fully stocked. Within a month, all the bottles from the bar were empty. It got to the point that Ronald drank himself to sleep and would pass out right on the floor every night. Since I didn't feel sorry for him, I left him right there nightly and stepped over his body, as if he was already dead.

Ronald drank so much that he would wake up the next morning, smelling and looking like he was still drunk. He was the CFO on the board of directors of the Cadillac dealership and he also owned two of the dealerships. He was dedicated to his work and provided a good living for our family. He had always traveled for business meetings. But after Mama died, he couldn't travel as much because there was no one to watch Mya and me. With technology, it was easy for him to Skype his meetings, allowing him to be home more. That turned out to be the worst thing for *him* and *us*. The more he was home, the more he drank. Eventually, his drinking started to affect his work.

There was a park two blocks away from our house. Mya and I went to the park and stayed most of the day just to avoid him. It was a small park with a two-sided swing set, one side for the babies and the other for the bigger kids. There was a long slide and tall monkey bars, which I had to pick Mya up for in order for her to swing on because she couldn't reach them by herself. In the play area, the ground was soft. So, if you fell off the monkey bars or the swings, you wouldn't hurt yourself. The park was clean and not many people visited it, so we were able to create a world of our own. That park became our haven. Sometimes, Gavin met us at the park. We would sit at the picnic table to do our homework and study for tests.

Because things at home were getting worse, we stopped going straight home from school. We would go to the park and stay there for as long as we could stand the cold in the winters. But, in the summers, it seemed like we never went home, unless it was raining. Sometimes we pretended that our mother was there with us and we talked with her. Mya told our mother that she had been bad in school and that the teacher had sent her out of class. I knew right then that we had to plan for our life. Everything our mother had built and instilled in us was slowly falling apart.

As time went on, Ronald's drinking was getting out of control. It was as if we didn't exist. He forgot we were mourning, just like he was. He didn't realize we were just kids who had lost their mother.

One day while we were in the park, I told Mya we would have to write out our plans, hopes and dreams. Going to the park every day, Mya and I had a lot of heart-to-heart talks. My sister was everything to me. I knew, since her father wasn't going to step up and take care of us, I had to do it.

One day, when we got home from the park, as soon as we hit the porch, we heard loud music and laughter. This was becoming the norm for our house.

I looked at Mya. She looked at me, and I said, "Stay close to me."

When I opened the door, there were three half-naked women in our house, dancing all around Ronald. He was so drunk that he didn't realize we had walked in. He didn't try to hide anything; he carried on as if we were part of their party. I rushed Mya out the living room as fast as I could. As we were walking past, I glanced down at the table and saw mirrors with white powder lines and pills all over the table. I couldn't believe he hadn't even tried to hide anything from us—not even the half-naked women.

When I got to the stairs, Ronald and I locked eyes. Sarcastically, he asked me, "You want some?"

When I said nothing, he responded, "Then get yo' little ass upstairs and don't worry about what grown folks are doing!"

I didn't know what types of drugs were on that table. I just knew I had to protect my little sister from the life we were being introduced to because life, as we knew it, was over. I took Mya upstairs to her room, hoping she wouldn't ask questions. I wasn't prepared to answer any. I was so angry. I started pacing the floor.

Mya sat down on her bed and began to cry. I stopped pacing, put my arm around her.

"We're going to be alright. I'm going to take care of everything," I told her. I had no clue what we were going to do, but I knew I had to be a big brother and show her I was in control. I got her things ready for her bath. After her bath, I brushed her hair and told her to get ready for bed. I hurried to take my bath so Mya wouldn't be by herself for a long period of time. I trusted no one who came into our house. I knew, eventually, I would have to face my fears of my bedroom. But every time I went into my room, it felt cold.

I remembered what I was taught. *Boys weren't supposed to cry. Real men don't cry. Crying was for girls and sissies.* So, instead of crying, I closed the door and decided to try praying again.

"Now I lay me down to sleep. I pray, my Lord, my soul to keep. I'm on my knees, just like you said. Lord, please remove these *spirits from my bed*."

I prayed to God that night, the next night, and many nights after that. I told God I needed Him to help me because I didn't know what to do. I didn't know how I was going to walk in my mother's footsteps. How was I going to raise my sister? I know I told God I would never praise Him again, so I figured this is why He didn't answer my prayers. I grew even more angrier with God.

Eventually, I stopped praying. Even though I really needed Him to tell me what to do, God never said a word. My mother and grandmother always said, "The Bible says, 'My sheep hear My voice.'" Well, obviously, I wasn't one of God's sheep because I didn't hear His voice. He had ignored me for so long—and our situation was getting worse and worse—that I no longer believed God was real. So, now, I knew I had to do this on my own.

I never forgot the events that took place in my bedroom. By now, there were some nights I managed to sleep in my room. But the nights I couldn't handle being in my room, I went into Mya's room and slept on the floor. Every time I woke up, she was right on the floor with me. Since the night our mom had died, Mya had never come into my room.

When she would wake up in the middle of the night, and I wasn't on the floor by her bed, she would come stand just outside my door. She would call my name until I woke up, then ask me to come sleep in her room. Every time she asked me, no matter how tired I was, I got up and went to her room.

Months had gone by when I noticed that Ronald wasn't going to work. He was no longer on any conference calls or leaving the house. The parties became more frequent and totally out of control. Women and men were coming and going all times of the day and night. We didn't know what was going on because Ronald didn't talk to us unless he was yelling at us. So, I made sure that we gave him nothing to yell about. The only time we had a home-cooked meal was when we ate at Gavin's house. Other than that, all Ronald bought were small, soggy burgers that always gave us gas. I told Mya, when we were older, we would never eat burgers again.

I later found out Ronald had lost his job due to his drinking and drug use. He was partying so much that he started going to work high. His performance became an embarrassment to the company, until finally, it cost him everything. Being the CFO, Ronald was the face of Cadillac. His face was in all the commercials, at the auto shows and at all the speaking engagements. He made all the important decisions when it came to the business needs of the company.

Ronald had plenty of chances to keep his job. When he was first suspended, he was sent to a drug treatment center for rehab. But it seemed like the more the company tried to help him, the worse his behavior became. Stories leaked to the press about the CFO doing drugs and having embarrassing sexual relations with women and men. The dealership didn't want the embarrassment of the bad press and Ronald stopped accepting the help they offered him. So, they forced him into early retirement. The dealership not only did it to save the reputation of the company, but they also did it because of the years Ronald had invested with the company and what he meant to the company. They let him go quietly, not making his drug use public. They made sure Ronald was well taken care of financially, as well.

After Ronald was released, his drug use got totally out of control. He became impossible to live with. Ronald's moves became so unpredictable that I knew I had to watch over and protect my baby sister. When we came home from school, I made sure we stayed out of his way. Mama had always stayed on us about keeping our rooms clean and keeping the bathroom clean. She always made sure we bathed and that our clothes were clean. I had to teach myself how to wash our clothes and clean like my mother used to do. I used to watch her as she separated the darks from the lights, then washed each load separately. But I didn't remember how she washed the clothes that had both light and dark colors. I messed up a few loads before I got it right, but I made sure our clothes were never dirty.

Another school year rolled around. Mya and I were now in the same school and, just like before, I made sure we got to school on time every day. I knew that would make my mother proud. I studied harder so I would always be able to help Mya with her schoolwork, projects and tests. Whenever I was uncertain about my own schoolwork, I had Mya stay after school with me while I got help. Things were so bad at home that I never wanted to leave Mya alone with him. With all the drinking, women and drugs, Ronald had become so detached from us that we were able to do whatever we wanted, if we didn't bother him. We didn't have a curfew. We had no structure, no discipline and no parental guidance. I knew we couldn't continue to live like that.

I told Mya we were having a family meeting at the park. We invited Gavin, since we were brothers from another mother. In our first meeting, we discussed our plans for our future. We first discussed what our mother had already taught us.

I said to Mya, "We're going to compile a list of Mama's rules and we're going to live by them."

Gavin suggested some of the rules his father and mother had laid down for him, and we wrote them all down and agreed to live by those rules.

After we read all the rules, Mya turned and asked a question I wasn't prepared for.

"Kyle, I know if I break the rules, I'll be in trouble with you. But if you break the rules, who are you going to be in trouble with?"

Gavin and I looked at each other. I started tickling Mya and said, "I don't plan on breaking any rules."

I knew right then that I had to be an example for my sister if she was going to respect me. Not only did I have to be fair with her, but I had to adhere to the rules, as well. I promised myself that I would be someone my sister could be proud of. Mya and I posted the rules in our rooms, and I read them every morning so I wouldn't forget them.

❧⋅⦿⦿⋅❧

Ronald was blowing so much money on sex and drugs that he had stopped paying attention to everything that mattered. He wasn't even taking care of our basic needs anymore. Mya and I came home one day, flipped the light switch, and the lights didn't come on. I thought something was wrong, but I didn't have a clue where to look.

I told Mya, "Let's make sure all the lights are screwed into their sockets."

Still nothing.

I noticed the unopened mail piled up in the kitchen. We started opening and reading it. After going through the stack of unopened mail, I realized the lights and gas had been shut off for non-payment. The mortgage hadn't been paid, in addition to a host of other bills that had piled up. I stood over Ronald, furious that he was passed out on the sofa. I knew I had to do something because we were on our way to being put out on the streets.

I went through Ronald's wallet and my mother's old purse. I got all the bank account information I could. Time had passed, but Ronald hadn't put any of my mother's things away. If you walked into our house, you would think my mother was still here because Ronald didn't change anything. That made it hard to grieve. Every day, it seemed as if my mother was still there, but she wasn't.

I took all the banking information and the bills to Mr. and Mrs. Washington so they could teach me how to pay them. We couldn't lose everything. I have always been secretive about what was going on in our house. So, I made up a story, telling them that my mother always handled all the bills. Jokingly, I said, "Ronald doesn't even know how to spell bills." I couldn't tell them how we were living because I was embarrassed. I also thought they would report Ronald to social services. After all, Mr. Washington was a lawyer and they loved Mya and me. I didn't want him to use his power because life for Mya and me could really change. We could possibly be split up. My job was to make sure Mya and I stayed together, and no one was going to jeopardize that.

Mr. and Mrs. Washington taught me how to pay the bills online. They helped me create passwords for the accounts I could pay online and taught me how to mail the other ones that I couldn't pay online. I quickly learned how to forge Ronald's name on the bottom of his checks. I also ordered a new debit card and set up a pin so I could have access to the money. I couldn't believe the balances my mom and Ronald had in their accounts. We weren't poor. Now I understood how Mama was able to host the big events. We lived in a great neighborhood. We had a huge home. Mom and Ronald both drove fancy cars, and we never wanted for anything.

Even though Ronald had been forced to retire from his job, he was able to cash in on his investments. What he got from the insurance money and other benefits was more than enough to take care of us. After my mom died, Mr. Washington applied for our mother's Social Security benefits. He had all the paperwork processed and set the money up to go directly into the custodial accounts my mother set up for us. He wanted to make sure Ronald didn't find out about the money. I believe Mr. Washington knew what was going on in our house, but he just went along with what I told him. He never questioned me when my explanations didn't make sense. However, he made sure we were always taken care of. With all the money going into our custodial accounts, by the time we were set to graduate from high school, we would be financially prepared to provide for ourselves. Ronald knew nothing about the money and nothing about us.

Ronald never inquired about us going to school, doing homework, or even what we ate for dinner. Most of the time, he didn't even know where we were. Gavin's mother went to the parent-teacher conferences in place of our parent because Ronald didn't give a crap about raising us. He was so stoned most of the time that it didn't even shock us anymore. Besides, we never gave our teachers any trouble. We always had good grades and behavior. So, there was never a reason to question what our home life was like. To others, it appeared that our home life was stable and good. However, it was far from it. When my mom died, we were at different schools. Therefore, none of our teachers had previously met our mom. Subsequently, teachers thought Mrs. Washington was our mother, and we never corrected them.

I did everything I could to make Mya believe we had just as good a life as all the other kids our age. I didn't want her to feel anything different. Mrs. Washington took us clothes shopping when she shopped for Gavin. Because she knew we had the Social Security money, she never questioned where we were getting the money from. She just assumed Ronald was making sure we had money. But it was me taking money from his account, making sure we never went without.

Many nights, Mya and I sat on the floor in her room, talking about how unhappy we were. We had a projector that showed stars on the wall. We would count the stars, making a wish on the last star. We remembered what our mother had told us: "Reach for the stars and never settle for less than all of them."

One night, we both wished Gavin's parents were our parents. By this time, so many women were passing through our house that we couldn't keep up with them. We made jokes about them and even called them our stepmothers. Our stepmothers came in different shapes and sizes. Some looked like streetwalkers, while others looked like diamond queens. I wondered why those beautiful women were here and, furthermore, why they were with him. No sooner than we started joking about it, it seemed like every other week we had a new stepmother. Sometimes, we had two or three stepmothers at a time. The only good thing about our stepmothers was that one of them usually cooked and I made sure we ate.

One night, I was laying Mya's pajamas out when one of our stepmothers came up the stairs. She watched silently, then asked me, "How did you learn to take care of your little sister like you do?"

I answered, "My mama taught me to always protect my sister."

She said, "Where is your mother?"

I responded, "She's dead. Ronald killed her."

Her eyes got big, but I could tell she thought I was just an angry kid. She paid what I said no mind and went back down the stairs.

It was almost time for bed, so I told Mya to get ready for her bath. At that time, Mya was about eleven. When she took her baths, I made sure she went into the bathroom with everything she needed. I told her never to come out the bathroom until she was fully dressed. I would stand in front of the door just to make sure no one walked in on her. There was so much sex, drugs and suspect men and women coming in and out of our home that I had to make sure my sister wasn't molested or raped.

While I was standing in front of the bathroom door waiting for Mya to come out, Ronald and our stepmothers came up the stairs. I could see all of them were high and drunk. They had been smoking and drinking since before we had come home from school. They were stumbling over one another and laughing profusely. One of my stepmothers looked at me and smiled. I didn't understand what she was smiling about, so I hurriedly looked away as they all stumbled into Ronald's room. The door slammed, and I heard them fall on the bed, continuously laughing.

I knocked on the bathroom door and whispered to Mya, "Hurry up!"

You never knew what was going to happen next in our house, but I was going to protect Mya at any cost. I tried to make sure she didn't see everything. Unfortunately, there were some things I couldn't shield her from.

When Mya came out of the bathroom, I followed her into her bedroom. I tucked her in every night, but she still had nights where she cried for Mama. I cried with her because I missed Mama, too. As I was tucking her in, we heard a loud thump, then laughter. There were a lot of weird noises coming from Ronald's room. Since Mya's room was directly across from his, she couldn't escape the sounds. I turned the radio on to drown out the sounds and let her know I would take care of everything.

I walked out of Mya's room and stared at Ronald's door as the noises grew more intense. I was so curious about the noises coming from Ronald's bedroom that I slowly cracked open his bedroom door. The smell coming from his room was the most awful thing I had ever smelled. The room was dark with a little light coming from a small lamp on the nightstand, which lit the room just enough for me to see what was going on.

I couldn't believe what I was seeing. I saw one stepmother sitting on Ronald's face. The second stepmother was straddling him, and the third stepmother was under them, licking in between his legs. My eyes grew bigger and bigger. The stepmother who had spoken to me earlier turned and looked me right in the eyes. Highly embarrassed, I slowly shut the door and ran to my room. I got into bed and tried to fall asleep as fast as I could, but my mind was so far away from sleeping. I was totally disturbed.

About twenty minutes later, I heard a hand grab my doorknob. The doorknob turned slowly, and the door opened. I felt the light shine across my face. I closed my eyes, pretending I was asleep, but stepmother knew I wasn't sleeping. She came in, stood right in front of me, and softly spoke my name. I opened my eyes.

Stepmother said, "I knew you weren't sleep."

She stood in front of me with a long, red satin robe on. She had short, curly hair. She was brown-skinned and tall. She reminded me of Halle Berry because she was so pretty. Her robe was opened in the front just enough for me to see that she had nothing on underneath. I wasn't sure why she came into my room. I was so scared. I just stared at the door because I thought Ronald would come looking for her. But I guess he was asleep from all the sex and drugs because he never came behind her.

Stepmother said to me, "I've been watching you."

I didn't make a sound. She closed the bedroom door and the room got dark. I couldn't see her, and she couldn't see me. The light came on and my eyes had to adjust from being in the dark. When I looked up, stepmother was standing over me with her vagina in my face. I looked down her long legs, and stepmother lifted my head with her finger. When she saw the terrified look on my face, she said, "Don't be scared."

Stepmother sat on my bed, took my hand and put it on her breast, and told me to squeeze. My hand was shaking as I touched her breast. I swallowed a big lump of saliva because I couldn't believe what was happening to me. Stepmother wore a crooked smile. She reeked of the same smell that had come from Ronald's room. She leaned in to kiss me, but I quickly moved away. I saw what she had been doing with her mouth with Ronald and the other stepmothers, and I wasn't letting her put her mouth on mine.

I was shaking. Stepmother told me to relax and let her show me how a man should be treated. I thought, *But I'm not a man! I'm just thirteen and a half!* Once again, I was trapped in my room. But this time, I knew my mother wasn't coming to rescue me. I didn't know where my rescue was going to come from this time. I just wanted stepmother to leave my room, but I couldn't speak. I was just as scared of her as I was of Ronald, but absolutely nothing could prepare me for what happened next.

Stepmother pulled back my sheets, leaned over my bed, and gave me a blowjob.

Chapter 3
Mya

Life for Kyle and me became difficult after Mama died. It seemed like my father had totally given up on life. He forgot that Kyle and I were just kids and that we were grieving, too. Grandma was so far away, and even though we talked to her often on the phone, Kyle didn't want her to worry about us. So, we made everything seem like it was fine when we spoke to her. She never suspected anything. We were never going to adapt to this horrific lifestyle with my father. So, Kyle and I made a promise that we would always raise our minds above our circumstances. We vowed that we would not be consumed by the things around us.

As a child, when you see so much and go through so much, you question if there is a God. So many nights, Kyle and I prayed for things to get better. When they didn't, we started thinking there wasn't a God. But that contradicted everything our mother and grandmother had taught us about Him. I became very confused about who God was and the power they said He has. I no longer understood the songs I sang as a child. There was no one here to explain them to me, so I looked to Kyle for wisdom. What did I know? I was just a kid. I didn't know anything about faith and long-suffering. I just wanted to be happy.

I used to love going to church with Mama and Grandma. I had been in the children's choir and my mother was our choir director. But living with Ronald, going to church wasn't even an option for us anymore. Ronald never went to church with my mother. In fact, I think he had only been to church twice in his life: once, when he *married* my mother, and once, when he *buried* my mother. Since God had let all this stuff happen to us, He had to have forgotten about us. So, what was the point in continually praying to Him? I felt like God was a mean God. I didn't believe He loved me. I didn't feel like He loved me, even though many songs tell me that He does.

Sometimes, I sat in the middle of my bed, singing *Jesus Loves Me*, just like my mother would sing to me. I could never forget that song because my mother and I would make up silly verses and laugh. Kyle would come in with his silly verse and he would do silly dances, and Mom would let us have fun. Mama would always say, "One day, you will sing this song and understand the true meaning of the words you're singing." Today wasn't that day. I didn't believe in it anymore.

My mother always sang to us. She was such a songbird. She would sing while we were washing dishes, cleaning the house, or when I was taking a bath. She would hit these high notes that made my eyebrows rise. She taught us that God watches over all His children.

So, I asked Kyle, "Why isn't God watching over us right now?"

Kyle always tried to make the best of things. So, he simply answered, "God's watching. It's just that there are other kids in worse situations than us. God has to take care of them first, but He's watching and He's coming."

He didn't really believe that. He just wanted to make me feel better. Kyle always knew how to make me smile and make me feel special.

He always tried to make our situation seem as if it wasn't as bad as it was. He told me that I was beautiful, smart and funny. Kyle really believed in building my self-esteem. He brought me fresh flowers and gifts, and he made sure I didn't have to ask anyone for anything. My brother and I had some of the deepest conversations, and we relied on each other so much. You didn't see him without seeing me.

Because of all the things taking place in our house, Kyle was always afraid of someone coming into my bedroom at night and touching me. So, some nights, he would get his sleeping bag and his pillow, and he slept right next to my bed on the floor. He always kept his blue and gray Louisville baseball bat he received on his birthday right by his side. Kyle was always my protection from the outside world. He told me that if anybody ever came into my room to hit them in their private part and scream. Then, he would come running. If I did not have my brother, I would have wanted God to kill me with my mother. My brother made me believe I could be anything I wanted to be in life. The only thing I was forbidden to be was a *stepmother*.

With everything my grandmother, mother and brother had instilled in me, there was no way I could even entertain the thought of living my life like the women who came through our house. And, as fast as the days were changing, so was my body. But there was no one there to explain why my chest hurt as my breasts got bigger. I was growing hair on my vagina and it seemed like my breasts just popped out overnight. I felt so insecure about my body that I wore big clothes so no one could see my shape. Baggy clothes were in style anyway, so I don't think Kyle even noticed.

Eventually, the biggest change of them all came. I woke up in the middle of the night, and my stomach was hurting so bad. I pulled my sheets back because I thought I'd wet the bed, but my sheets were full of blood. I immediately started crying and I yelled for Kyle. Kyle came running in my room like a superhero with his Louisville Slugger.

"What's wrong? What's wrong, Mya! What's wrong?"

I pulled the sheets back. Kyle saw the blood and he immediately panicked.

"Mya, where did you cut yourself?"

"I didn't cut myself."

"Then, where are you bleeding from?"

There was an awkward silence. We both looked down at my private area at the same time. I was filled with embarrassment and neither of us knew what to do. Kyle paused for a moment, then he ran out the room. Kyle grabbed towels from the linen closet, and he wrapped them around me like a diaper. I sat there, looking like a fourteen-year-old infant, while Kyle paced the floor, wondering what he should do.

Being such a naïve girl, I asked, "Kyle, why don't we call 9-1-1? I have to go to the hospital to stop the bleeding."

Kyle paused, took a deep breath, and responded, "No, Mya. It's called a period, but I don't know what to do."

I yelled, "Well, we need to do something because I have blood running down my leg."

My humiliation was growing. I knew I couldn't just sit on the bed. I wasn't sure what to do. All I could think was, *If my mother was here, she would know exactly what to do*. I started to cry.

Kyle said, "Mya, stop crying because I'm not going to hold you; you'll get blood all over me."

"Kyle, it's not funny; do something!"

Kyle knew he had to act fast. He ran out the room and brought back another towel. Finally, he came up with an idea. I never questioned Kyle because he always had the best answers, but I should have known he was going to call on Mrs. Washington. Kyle grabbed my hand. We went across the street and knocked on the Washingtons' door. It was 4:30 in the morning.

Mr. Washington opened the door in a panic because he thought something was wrong. I could see Mrs. Washington standing behind him, looking on. When he looked down and saw me wrapped in towels with a big sheet around me, Mr. Washington immediately said, "Baby, Mya needs you." Mr. Washington told us to come in.

Mrs. Washington took one look at me and knew exactly what was wrong. She took me into the bathroom, ran some bath water, and told Kyle to go back across the street to get some clean clothes and underclothes for me. Then she turned to me and said, "If you're uncomfortable and want me to leave, I'll leave."

I replied, "No, please don't leave me."

I got undressed. Mrs. Washington wiped the blood off my legs, I got in the tub, and she threw the bloody towels and my pajamas away. I told Mrs. Washington how embarrassed I was about my body developing.

Mrs. Washington chuckled and said, "I was wondering why you were looking as if you were wearing Kyle's clothes."

Mrs. Washington kneeled on the side of the tub. As she took the washcloth and poured water down my back, she started singing *Jesus Loves Me* just like my mother used to sing to me. Mrs. Washington sung in the choir with my mother, and that was their favorite song. They used to sing that song together and the church would go crazy over their rendition. I started to cry because, at that moment, I felt my mother's presence all over me. I felt as if my mother was singing to me through Mrs. Washington. My mind drifted as she was singing. I heard my mother's voice say, "I'm proud of you and your brother. Don't you ever doubt God."

I cried so hard in that bathtub. I felt like I was releasing some of the anger I had been carrying since my mother had passed away.

Mrs. Washington said, "It's okay, Mya. Let it out. I miss her, too."

It was as if she knew why I was crying. I missed my mother so much. I needed her more than ever. But she wasn't there. Mrs. Washington was, and she felt like my mother right then. I was okay that Mrs. Washington was sharing this moment with me. She told me I was becoming a young woman, and it was time for her and me to have the young woman talk. Mrs. Washington called into work that morning and she told Kyle she was keeping me home from school.

She showed me how to properly care for myself when my cycle started. We went for hot apple cider and she explained becoming a woman to me. I told Mrs. Washington I was embarrassed by my body because my breasts were growing, my hips were spreading, and hair was growing in dark places. She told me that my body was beautiful. She reminded me how beautifully built my mother was. It looked like I was going to be built the same way. My mother was beautiful, and she had a very shapely body. Everywhere we went, men always took a double look at her. However, I wasn't sure if I could ever walk with the poise and grace that my mother had. She lit up a room whenever she walked in.

Mrs. Washington and I spent the whole day together. She took me to Victoria's Secret, had my body measured, and bought me my first matching bra-and-panty set. Since we were at the mall, she said, "Let's also get you some clothes that fit."

Mrs. Washington made sure I was prepared for my cycle for at least the next six months. She also bought me the most stylish outfits to complement my body. When we were done shopping, I had plenty of pretty bra-and-panty sets, plenty of sanitary napkins, and a few outfits that would surely make everyone look twice at me. It felt good to have a woman who cared about me just as much as my mother did. I felt like I was Mrs. Washington's daughter.

When I got back to school, everyone was so used to me wearing baggy clothes that, when they saw my new look, my girlfriends were amazed, and the boys looked hard.

Even Kyle said, "What did Mrs. Washington do to you?"

I had to own the new look. So, I took on a new personality, but I was determined to learn everything I could about a woman's body. I didn't understand the changes I was experiencing. So, I went to the library and checked out my first anatomy book. I read that book from cover to cover.

The library had a whole section on the anatomy of the male and female body. Every week, I checked out a different anatomy book. Before l knew it, I'd read so many anatomy books that I dreamed of becoming an anatomy professor. I never wanted any other girl to experience what I'd gone through. I wanted to educate girls about their bodies. That created a huge new dream for me. No longer did I dream of just getting away from my father.

Kyle did everything he could to shelter me from what was going on in our house, but he couldn't shield me from everything. One Saturday night, my father was on his drunken tangent. As usual, he had several people in our home. I didn't think my father even knew I was home. I was in my room when I heard a bunch of noise coming from the living room. I knew what those noises meant because we were used to them. But it didn't stop me from becoming angry. I thought I would finally give my father a piece of my mind. I opened my bedroom door and stormed down the stairs, thinking I was getting ready to confront the situation. But this was the moment when my life drastically changed—again.

I ran downstairs to the living room and I couldn't believe what I saw. My father was so high that I don't think he even knew he was receiving fellatio from a man. Two stepmothers were on the opposite sofa, having sex with one another. Another stepmother was bending over, kissing my father in the mouth. When she looked up at me, I couldn't move. I stood there, paralyzed, with tears in my eyes. My mother had to have turned over in her grave at least one hundred times.

Everyone was as naked as the day they were born. One stepmother walked over to the cocktail table, grabbed a mirror with white powder on it, walked over to me and said, "Would you like to try some and join us?"

I just stood there. I couldn't believe she was offering me drugs and sex with my own father. My father was so stoned that he didn't even realize I was in the room. She grabbed my breast and put her mouth on top of my shirt.

She looked at me and said, "Hold this. I'm going to take your clothes off."

I couldn't believe my eyes or ears, and I still couldn't move. I was terrified of what I had walked into. Stepmother handed me the mirror with the powder on it. I took it, still unable to move. I wasn't even supposed to be there. I was supposed to be at the playground, waiting for Kyle. I looked at the white powder.

Stepmother said, "Let me show you how to do it." She took the straw, put it up to her nose, and snorted the white powder off the glass.

As her eyes rolled in the back of her head, I stood there, holding the mirror and shaking. As I watched her, she got higher. I looked at the mirror, my mind racing. I thought, *If I get high like them, I won't feel this pain anymore.* I watched as stepmother's body moved seductively. She came toward me and tried to kiss me. I pushed her away, still overcome by fear.

Then, I heard the key in the front door. The lock turned and the door opened. Kyle was standing in the doorway. He saw me holding the mirror with the powder on it. At first, I wasn't breathing. But when I saw Kyle, I breathed, and the tears fell. The rage that came over Kyle was like nothing I had ever seen before. Kyle ran over to me and knocked the mirror across the room, shattering it. The look of disgust that came over his face made me fall to my feet, crying.

Kyle grabbed me and started shaking me, yelling, "What did you do? What did you? You were supposed to wait at the park. I went to the park, Mya, but you weren't there! You were supposed to wait at the park!"

Kyle was so upset that he could barely get his words out. I saw the pain in his face as he gasped for air and asked me, "What did you do? Did they make you take this shit?"

Finally, I snapped out of the trance. I yelled, "Kyle, I didn't do anything! I didn't do anything! I promise, Kyle! I'm sorry, Kyle. I'm sorry!"

Kyle never wanted me home alone with my father. If we were ever separated, I was either supposed to wait at the park, or go to Gavin's house and wait for him there. Then, we would come home together.

Kyle yelled again, "You were supposed to wait at the park for me! Is this what you want? You want to be one of *them*?"

My father finally realized Kyle and I were in the room. He jumped up to grab his pants, hurried to put them on, then yelled at Kyle. "Get your hands off my daughter!"

Kyle turned and told everyone, "Get out!"

At first, everyone looked around. But when Kyle said it again in a tone that meant he was getting ready to hurt someone, everyone ran to put their clothes on. Ronald made the mistake of yelling at Kyle.

"You can't put anyone out of my house! This is my house! Who the hell are you?"

Kyle didn't say a word. He leaped across the room at Ronald and tackled him to the floor. They started fighting like two grown men on the street. I was so terrified; I had never seen that side of Kyle. I was too scared to call the police because, with all the drugs on the table, Ronald would surely have gone to jail. I screamed at them to stop, but they kept fighting until Kyle hit my father so hard that he fell through the living room glass table, shattering it.

Kyle looked at me. I looked at my father, who was just lying there. He didn't even try to get up. I thought Kyle had killed my father. I got ready to check if my father was okay, but Kyle was so angry that he snatched my arm, dragged me up the stairs, and yelled at me. This was more than anger. There was deep hurt and confusion. He seemed so displaced. Kyle had never raised his voice at me. But when he threw me on my bed and yelled at the top of his lungs, I knew he had reached his boiling point.

"You are *never* supposed to come home without me! This is what I've been trying to protect you from!"

"Kyle, I wasn't going to do anything. I promise."

Kyle yelled back at me, "Shut up! Just shut up, Mya! They would have *made* you do it! Is this what you want? Come on then. Let's do it together. Let's let all our hopes and dreams blow up in smoke. What do you think I've been protecting you from? What were you doing in their faces anyway?"

I couldn't say anything. I just sat there, crying, because I had disappointed my brother. As Kyle paced back and forth, he was trying to figure out our next move. I was trying to stop crying. Kyle never liked it when I cried. When he finally looked at me and saw how broken I was, all his defenses came down. He grabbed me, put his arms around me, and said, "I can't lose you, Mya. Mama's depending on me to take care of you. You have to listen to me. All I've got is you!" I saw a tear roll down my brother's face. "I can't lose you, Mya. You're the reason I keep going."

I couldn't take this. I knew I had hurt him badly. The only thing I could do was to keep telling him, "I'm sorry." I never wanted to disappoint my brother.

Kyle grabbed our suitcases and overnight bags. He told me to get everything I wanted because we were never coming back.

"What? Kyle, where are going to go?"

"Mya, I don't know yet. But we can't live this type of life anymore. I can't risk them getting to you."

I wasn't going to challenge him in that moment. So, we got everything we could carry and went to the park. I sat on our bench, crying, while Kyle held me. I was crying so hard that Kyle yelled out, "Mama, please tell us what to do! We're lost without you. Where is the God you taught us about? Why hasn't He come?"

Kyle and I stayed at the park for a few hours. It was getting late and we started to get hungry. I was looking to Kyle for direction.

Kyle said, "Get your stuff. Let's go."

We went to Gavin's house. Kyle and I had always said we would never tell what was going on in our house. But the time had come when we had to explain why we were running away from Ronald. Kyle sat down and told Mr. and Mrs. Washington everything.

Without hesitation, Gavin's parents allowed us to stay with them. Gavin's parents were lawyers. They owned their own law firm. I begged them not to bring any charges against my father. Although life with my father hadn't been great, I still loved him. I was glad to be away from him, but I didn't want him to be prosecuted. I knew we could never go back there again. I swore to Kyle I would graduate with honors, and I would make Mama and him proud of me.

Mrs. Washington prepared the guest room for me in their huge five-bedroom home. Kyle was going to share a room with Gavin. Gavin and Kyle were best friends and thought that was the best arrangement ever. One room was used as the Washingtons' home office, and it was full of law books. The Washingtons' home was like our home, so we knew our way around. However, Kyle told Mrs. Washington that he was going to sleep in the guest room with me tonight.

After everyone was settled and The Washingtons went to sleep, Kyle and I had a long conversation about what had happened. He explained why he was so upset. If I thought Kyle was overprotective before, I hadn't seen anything yet.

Kyle and Gavin made sure that no boy in school even *thought* about talking to me. Word got around that they beat up a boy in my class for hitting me on the butt. That made all the other boys not want to deal with Kyle or Gavin. No boy in high school talked to me. My body was developing so fast. My breasts showed through my shirts and my butt was very noticeable. My body became the main attraction of our high school, but Mrs. Washington always made sure I was dressed like a young lady.

She said, "Your mother was a looker in high school, too. You get your body from her."

The clothes Mrs. Washington bought me always made me feel pretty. It wasn't long before that prettiness went to my head. I knew I was the next best thing going. Even when I flirted with different guys, none of them would talk to me because of Kyle and Gavin. If they caught a boy eyeballing me, they would threaten him and tell him he'd better stay a football field's length away from me. My high school years were turning out to be my most miserable years, but that would soon change.

Kyle was a senior in high school, and Gavin and I were both in the tenth grade. One night, Kyle was out with some friends, doing senior stuff. Gavin and I were in his room, talking about the current events at school like we always did.

The tenth grade dance was coming up, and neither Gavin nor I had a date. Kyle wouldn't let me go with any of the guys at school anyway. So, I was mocking him in front of Gavin.

"I'll be damned if any of the boys are going to turn you into a stepmother. I'll go to jail first!"

Gavin and I laughed about Kyle's overprotectiveness. But he couldn't laugh too hard because he was overprotective, too.

I asked Gavin, "Why don't you have a date for the dance?"

He replied, "I do have a date."

This shocked me because I didn't know Gavin was seeing someone. I responded, "What stanky girl are you taking to the dance?"

Gavin replied, "First off, she doesn't stank. Second, she's the baddest girl in the school."

I yelled out, "Are you talking about Renee? Ugh!"

Renee was another girl all the boys couldn't keep their eyes off, and she couldn't keep her hands off them. Her reputation preceded her.

"That girl sleeps with everyone. Besides, she isn't the baddest girl in the school. The baddest girl in the school would be you, and I'm taking you to the dance."

Go figure. Going to the dance with Gavin would be like going to the dance with Kyle. I responded, "Well, it isn't like Kyle is going to let me go with any other guy anyway."

Gavin said, "You don't get it, do you?"

"Get what, Gavin?"

Gavin leaned in and tried to kiss me. I pulled away because I had never been kissed before. Gavin grabbed me and pulled me closer to him. He stared into my eyes and told me to trust him. He leaned in again, pressed his lips against mine, and I remembered what I had read in my anatomy books. I slightly opened my mouth and let him gently put his tongue into my mouth. I moved my tongue backward and forward in his mouth. He was moving his tongue in my mouth, as well. I was kissing for the very first time, and it was with Gavin.

I always kept my crush on Gavin to myself because we were so close growing up. Besides, I didn't want to mess up Kyle and Gavin's friendship. If Kyle found out about our kiss, I knew it would surely destroy their friendship. Kyle didn't want anyone touching me, but it sure felt good. Gavin was so fine, so gentle and so passionate. My body was ready to do whatever he told it to do.

There were so many girls at school who were in love with Gavin. They all flocked around him like he was a celebrity. I always thought he would date one of the more popular girls because he was so popular. Gavin always treated me like Kyle treated me—like I got on his nerves. But

I guess it was his cover-up because I was kissing him and there were so many girls who would have loved to be in my shoes.

After kissing Gavin multiple times, I asked him, "What does this mean?"

Gavin looked at me and said, "This means, from now on, you're my lady."

I said, "Gavin, this isn't good. What about Kyle? This will surely ruin your friendship. Please don't tell Kyle about this."

Gavin laid me down on his bed, kissed my lips, kissed my cheek, and whispered in my ear, "Don't worry. Kyle already knows."

The next time I kissed Gavin, we heard the front door open. Thank you, God, because I was ready to be Gavin's *stepmother*, but his parents came home.

Chapter 4
Mya

Gavin meant exactly what he said on the day we kissed. Kyle and Gavin had already spoken about us dating many times before, but I never heard about it until now. Gavin proved to Kyle that he really wanted to be with me. I guess Kyle was convinced. If Kyle had known I'd always had a crush on Gavin, I wondered if he would have chosen for us to move in with Gavin and his parents.

Gavin was a real upstanding guy, but we were also teenagers. He wanted to be just like his father, a lawyer. So, he emulated his father in the way he spoke, the way he handled situations, and the way he treated people. Gavin treated me like his father treated his mother, and I always felt special because of it. Kyle knew Gavin wasn't going to mistreat me or use me for sex. So, he was okay with us dating. Gavin was probably the only guy Kyle would ever have approved of me dating.

I had been so angry with Kyle because I barely could talk to any boys in school or outside of school. It was probably a good thing because it seemed like almost every boy who I thought I liked ended up with a baby with one of the popular girls. One boy I liked beat his girlfriend up in front of the whole school. Kyle wasn't going for a boy putting his hands on me.

After Gavin and I went to the dance together, I quickly became the talk of the whole school. I received so many dirty looks from the girls in school because so many of them had wanted to be with Gavin—not only because he was handsome—but because he was smart and loving. The girls loved him. Gavin wasn't promiscuous like Kyle. What I didn't know was that Gavin was still a virgin, too. I thought Gavin had had sex with at least one of the girls from school, but he hadn't. Everyone else also thought Gavin was just like Kyle when it came to the ladies, but he wasn't. He was guilty by association.

Kyle made it no secret that he was a ladies' man. He even had girls who got into fist fights over him at school. Some girls whom Kyle wouldn't pay any attention to tried to be my friend, thinking that would get them next to Kyle. However, it never worked. If Kyle wanted you, Kyle got you. But Gavin was different. Gavin treated me like I was the only woman in the world. Some of the girls liked me when they thought I was just Gavin's best friend's little sister. But once we started dating, it seemed as if everyone turned on me.

Being Gavin's girl and Kyle's sister surely had its advantages and disadvantages. I loved the protection, but sometimes, I felt like I was in jail. All the boys were scared to talk to me because Kyle was a hot head, and most of the girls wanted Gavin. Girls pretended to be my friend just to get close to me, so they could try to steal Gavin right out from under my nose. I became the popular girl no one wanted to be around.

Gavin talked me into signing up for the debate team. Debating was Gavin's field and he was good at it. Gavin planned to walk in his father's footsteps and become a lawyer, so this class was right up his alley. I signed with him, not knowing I would later love debating, like he did. It didn't take long for us to become a debate team. We debated against the other teams in our class and won every debate we competed in.

The following year, we continued the debate team and became the debate team champions of the school. This also made us captains of our debate team. Gavin and I created a strong team of debaters. We were so good that our teacher entered us into debate competitions with other schools. By participating in the debate competitions, we created quite the name for ourselves, winning trophy after trophy. We were so good that we started debating on a college level. We won many argumentative dissertations, arguments of persuasions and case studies. You name it, Gavin and I won it.

Once everyone got used to seeing Gavin and me as a couple, more people accepted and liked me. There were a few girls who still didn't like me because I had Gavin, but they didn't matter. We were named the most ideal couple and the couple most likely to succeed. We became the power couple of the school.

Sometimes, life doesn't go as planned. My dreams of becoming an anatomy professor were slowly put on the back burner as Gavin and I became more popular. I must admit, I fell in love with all the attention. I was pursuing Gavin's dream with him.

Our last year of high school, we were both in the running for valedictorian. We had college recruiters from all over pursue us because of our grades. We got acceptance letters from colleges we hadn't even applied to. I held a 4.3 GPA, and Gavin held a 4.1 GPA. I always held that over his head. Our GPAs were really the same, but I had taken an extra class. That made my GPA slightly higher than his.

But we weren't prepared for the biggest challenge of our life when it came. Yale, the most prestigious law school in the country visited our school. They gave debate teams a chance to be awarded full-ride scholarships to their university. They heard about our school's debate team, and our whole school was excited about the opportunity. This was what Gavin had prepared for his whole life. It meant more to him because his father was an alumnus of this prestigious university, which put Gavin one step closer to his dream. Mr. Washington was familiar with the challenge they were offering, and he was more than happy to assist in getting our debate team prepared for the challenge.

The whole debate team was put to the test, but only the best was going to represent the school. After all the challenges were over, only three of us were standing—Gavin, another student and me— and we were off to represent our school.

Gavin's parents helped us with our persuasive arguments as we planned to face off against the other high school teams that had won at the debate challenge previously. However, we had one thing in our corner they didn't have: an experienced alumnus of the school. That didn't mean we didn't have to study or prepare. It just meant we had more to live up to than everyone else.

The day came for the big face-off, and we were in a huge auditorium that was packed with people. There wasn't a seat left in the place. We were stationed on the floor in a half circle with the judges' table facing the contestants. There were also huge screens for the people who were sitting up high to see. Gavin's parents were there, of course. Kyle was there, and Grandpa and Grandma came all the way from Chicago. All the administrators from our school were there, and it seemed as if all of Detroit had shown up to support us.

Gavin seemed calm and collected. The other contestant and I were shaking in our shoes. The first debate came up. Our colleague froze in the middle of the debate. I jumped in, trying to save the debate. But she had already damaged us. We lost that debate. I leaned over and told her to let Gavin lead. We would support his arguments because Gavin was the stronger opponent. We were a team, but we would be awarded individual scholarships based on our knowledge and performance.

Our teammate wanted to take over the whole debate. I couldn't believe she was trying to be a show-off. She continued to go off subject. The judges warned her about her debate tactics. Finally, Gavin took over and shut her down because, at the rate she was going, we were going to lose the whole competition. We defeated all the opponents. Then, the debate of our life came. After defeating all the high schools, it was time to debate Yale's freshman class. I was so intimidated because they attended Yale. But Gavin's dad had prepared us for this. If we followed his strategy, we knew we would be successful. It was going to be a tough debate. We had to pull our teammate to the side and explain to her that we were in this together. We told her not to upstage us because we would lose the whole competition. It was so quiet in the auditorium that you could hear a mouse run across the floor. The debate started and, to my surprise, our teammate stuck right by our side. After winning four debates in a row, we won a grand total of five debates, with only one loss. It was enough to win the whole competition.

All three of us were awarded full-ride scholarships to the most prestigious law school in the country. That was the start of Gavin's dreams. The auditorium went wild. It was so loud in the auditorium that we couldn't hear ourselves congratulate each other. We were ecstatic. Everyone was happy that our school won the competition, and we became the superstars of our high school.

That year, the school elected to have both a male and a female valedictorian. No one wanted to choose between the two of us. We both had a stellar four years of high school. At one time, the teachers thought we were cheating, so they put us in different classes. It didn't matter. We were both determined to be the best we could be in high school.

Gavin gave the male valedictorian speech, and I gave the female valedictorian speech. We walked across the stage and received our diplomas together. Gavin and I had done it. We celebrated the whole night with Kyle and some good friends. We were off to college together, and my life was just beginning.

Years Later . . .

Chapter 5
KYLE

I ordered a gourmet dinner from The London Chop House. I popped a four-hundred-dollar bottle of Dom Perignon Rosé, limited edition. Fresh California strawberries enhanced the taste. Soft music filled the room. I dimmed the lights and lit two scented candles to create a nice aroma in the air. My table was set for two and the mood was just right. Sex was in the air.

My philosophy was that all women are lonely, and all you have to do is be different than the last man. Show a little cash, and they'll love you like you were their daddy. Most of the women I've slept with only slept with me because they knew I had money and I'd spend it on them. If the pussy's good, I'll pay for it. It's nothing for me to make a woman think I've spent a whole lot of money on her when she's just one of my budget hoes.

Budget hoes are women I treat according to the way they look, talk and act. Every woman has a budget. For the low-budget hoe, if I spend just a dollar more than what she's used to, I can manipulate her until I get sick of her, then throw her away. I've also made it harder for the next man to follow in my footsteps. I've gotten to the point where I've outgrown the low-budget hoes. They're becoming too much of a project. I've set my sights on higher-class budget hoes.

Let me *re-introduce* myself. My name is Kyle Lamar Johnson, Sr., and I'm twenty-six now. I'm a self-made man. I graduated from Morehouse, a historical black college in

Atlanta, Georgia, with a Bachelor of Business Law. I received my Master's in Accounting. I knew I wanted to be a business owner. I have a problem with authority, and I'm known for being the boss.

I am a very successful, high-end jewelry business owner. I own my own home and cars, and I'm incapable of loving a woman, but I love women. I love the way they taste, the way they smell, the way they look, and the way they fall all over me. I have a six-year-old son named of Kyle Lamar Johnson, Jr.; we call him Kyle Jr. After his mother broke my heart by leaving me, I promised myself I would never love another woman.

Kyle Jr.'s mother's name is Naomi, and she is truly the only woman I've ever loved. She is so close to the image I have of my mother—sweet, kind, loving, loyal, gentle—not to mention the fact that she believes in God and she's beautiful. If she ever gave me another chance, I would love to marry her, without thinking twice about it. But I have too many demons I'm fighting to be the husband she needs me to be. I try to cover up my inconsistencies by being a successful man. But no matter how much success I obtain, I can never escape my inability to deal with or understand my volatile actions when it comes to women. Unfortunately, I have concluded that I'm just a messed-up man.

Tonight, I put all that behind me as I sit across from a woman named Lisa. Lisa works for me. She's my administrative assistant and she's good at her job. She's also just like all the other women in my store: she wants to see what *The Kyle Experience* is about. She is one of the higher-class budget hoes because this woman is fine and educated. She has a body that would make even another woman take a double look. Lisa is a little snobby and her sexiness has gone to her head. She thinks quite a bit of herself, which I think is attractive because I'm completely full of myself.

As we giggled through dinner, we did more talking than I would originally do. Stepmother taught me to get straight to the point. Don't beat around the bush. Get that blowjob, make that woman cum hard, and send her away. I grabbed both wine glasses, invited Lisa over to the sofa, and set the wine glasses on the table. I've always believed in being a gentleman. So, I listened to her talk for just a little while longer.

When I got tired of listening to her, I stuck my tongue between her sweet pink lips. I heard her moan as my kiss turned her on. I laid her back on the sofa and eased my hands under the bottom of her shirt, working my way up to her breasts. I squeezed them firmly. I make my way to the inside of her bra to feel her nipples. I unbuttoned her shirt and sucked her sweet breasts, making her gasp for air. Her body moved to the same rhythm as mine, and I wanted to hit every point on her body.

Even though this woman had given me head on several occasions in my office after everyone else had left for the day, she knew I wanted her badly. She knew exactly what she was doing, switching through my office, teasing me with that body for months. I don't know why I never bent her over my desk. But tonight, it was time for me to give her exactly what she came over for. I unbuckled my pants, ready to make this woman another notch on my belt. I was ready to take her into my bedroom for a night she would never forget.

I whispered softly in her ear, "Baby, would you like to follow me to my bedroom?"

She looked me in my eyes and seductively said, "Yes, Kyle."

From across the room, I heard little footsteps running. I jumped up as Kyle Jr. stood over the back of the sofa yelling, "Daddy! Daddy! I'm scared. I had a bad dream and I already called Mommy. She's on her way to tuck me in."

My dick was standing up, hard as a train, in front of my son. Both Lisa and I were trying to fix our clothes. I prayed that Kyle Jr. didn't see her breasts. I held my head down and yelled, "Junior, go back to your room!"

Jr. stood in front of me and said, "I'm not leaving until my mother gets here."

Of all nights, he decided to be rebellious and talk back—which is not normal behavior for him. I put my hand on my belt buckle and told him, "If you don't get back in that room, I'm going to take my belt off and tear your little butt up!"

Kyle Jr. turned to go back to his room. Just before he left the living room, he shouted, "It looks like you were going to take your belt off anyway."

My son had never embarrassed me like this. He never talked back to me. I stood there, shocked. I knew I would have to deal with him later, but for now, I wanted to rekindle the mood so I could do what I set out to do. I apologized to Lisa, hoping I could get her back in the mood. I tried to pick up where we left off, but Lisa was stuck on the fact that Kyle Jr. said his mother was on the way. So, thanks to my son, I knew I'd have to work a little harder to get sex from this woman.

I told Lisa, "His mother coming over has nothing to do with you or what we're going to do in my bedroom. If she's in the bedroom putting Jr. to sleep, she'll never even know you're here. Naomi is just going to put Jr. back to sleep, then leave." I found myself trying to do more convincing than I ever have with any woman. Any moment now, I was going to tell Lisa to bounce; I could call someone else. Suddenly, there was a knock at the door.

Lisa stopped in her tracks, looked at me, and said, "I told you I should have left."

I said, "Girl, she'll be gone in a minute."

I walked over and slowly opened the door. There stood my college sweetheart, the mother of my one and only son. She was five-foot-five, with long, pretty black flowing hair with blonde streaks. She had caramel skin, a nice build, and a pink-and-black jogging suit with matching gym shoes. This woman took my breath away every time I saw her. I was a fool for not committing to her. She was my weakness. As I saw her standing here, in my mind, I wondered if I could have both tonight. But I knew Naomi would never go for that.

When Naomi entered and saw Lisa, she immediately got angry. She looked at me with that same look she had the night she caught me with another woman. Lisa politely excused herself to leave. As mad as Naomi looked, I wanted to leave right along with Lisa. After I closed the door behind Lisa, an uncomfortable silence filled the air. I could barely hold my head up to look at Naomi.

Angrily, Naomi said, "Where's Kyle Jr.?"

I tried to be a little flirty to break the tension. "You can't say hello?"

"Hello, Kyle. Where's my son?"

"Our son is in his room."

Naomi turned and I watched as she walked out the living room. Her hips switched from left to right, her butt filling out that jogging suit she was wearing. She knew I was watching. I felt like a little boy who wanted to do it to his first love for the first time. While she was in Kyle Jr.'s room, I hurriedly moved the wine glasses from the table and sprayed air freshener. I unbuttoned my pants, sat back on the sofa, and put one leg up. I rested my arm on the back of the couch, waiting for her to walk back into the living room.

When she entered the living room, she angrily asked, "What game are you two playing? Kyle Jr. is asleep."

Although I knew Naomi was mad when she entered the room, I clapped my hands twice and the sounds of Earth, Wind & Fire came softly through the speakers. I got up from the sofa, walked seductively over to her, and grabbed her by the hips. I turned her around, pinned her against the wall, and pressed her butt firmly against my genital area. I knew this would turn her on.

I whispered in her ear, "We aren't playing games. Jr. was awake, but now he's asleep."

I slowly kissed the back of her neck and felt her body relax. I turned her back around, picked her up, wrapped her legs around my waist, and carried her over to the sofa. I laid her down and kissed her cheeks, then her lips. She didn't hesitate to kiss me back. I knew just what to do to turn Naomi on. It didn't take much because she was still in love with me. I reminded her of how I was her first and how I used to make her feel when we made love. I knew if I got into her mind that her body would be sure to follow.

Naomi wasn't like the other women I've dealt with. She was my one true love. The more we touched, the harder I became and the more I wanted to get inside her. She responded so seductively, telling me that she remembered how I used to make her body feel. She remembered how it felt when I would first stick it in her. I was so aroused that I thought my dick was going to bust right through my pants.

I unbuttoned my pants, pulled my dick out, and said, "Girl, I want you so badly." I went to pull her jogging pants down, but she stopped me dead in my tracks.

"You want me as much as you wanted that woman who just left out of here? Get off me!"

I stuttered because I was stunned. I didn't know where *this* Naomi came from. She turned from a calm, docile woman into a mean, snarly woman in seconds. The strength she used to throw me off her felt like she had been lifting weights. I was totally shocked because Naomi always gave into me. I didn't understand the rejection. That's when the argument started.

She reminded me of why we broke up in the first place. I listened while she talked because, in a way, I felt like I deserved everything she was saying to me. Unfortunately, I just couldn't give Naomi what she needed. So, I let her vent—until she told me I was acting like an unfit father. That's where I drew the line. Naomi may not have liked the fact that I kept the company of a lot of women, but I was a wonderful father to my child.

Mya and Kyle Jr. were the only two people I trusted with my heart because I knew they were the only two people who had a pure, unadulterated love for me. Most people love with conditions. My son and Mya loved me, no matter what. That's the kind of love I needed. Naomi knew how to anger me, and she was really pushing me to the limit. I still loved Naomi and there were some boundaries I simply would not cross with her, no matter how hurtful her words were. I simply grabbed a pillow and blanket and threw them in her face.

I told her, "Look, it's very late. If you want to stay, you can sleep on the couch. If not, you can see yourself out."

I turned and walked away, heading to bed with my dick still hard.

Chapter 6
Mya

Gavin and I were on a full-ride scholarship at the law school we both attended. We were in our last year, one semester from graduation, when I couldn't go on any longer. I was completely burnt out. I was conflicted because I lived in a world that Kyle and Gavin created for me. This life wasn't working for me anymore.

Kyle always told me what to think, what to wear, when to stand up and sit down. All my life, I'd done what Kyle wanted me to do. I truly thanked him for the structure and his guidance. But now, I felt like I needed to think for myself. I knew I was intelligent. I graduated from high school with honors. I was on the Dean's List at Yale, but I didn't think for myself. It was time for me to figure my life out. So, I finally decided to leave the university.

I moved back home and got a place of my own, where I never stayed because I was always at Kyle's. Unfortunately, I left school without a plan. Kyle was shocked and disappointed that I left school so close to graduation. I tried to explain to him how I felt, but I could still tell how disappointed he was in me. After our conversation, and Kyle's normal lecture, Kyle made me promise to go back and finish what I started. At the very least, I had to start something new. I just couldn't quit. I knew Kyle had worked too hard for me just to quit. So, I had to figure out my plan.

One day, I was at Kyle's place hanging out. I heard a knock at the front door. It startled me because I wasn't expecting anyone. As I walked to the door, there was a second knock. This time, the knock was a little more aggressive.

"Hold on; I'm coming."

That second knock let me know the person on the other side of the door wasn't a stranger. However, I wasn't prepared for who was on the other side of the door.

I asked, "Who is it?"

There was no response.

I looked out the peephole, took a deep breath, and slowly exhaled. I open the door and paused. There he stood— six-one, light-skinned, haircut to the tee, with a hairline that was so straight it could cut through paper. His beard was trimmed to perfection. He wore black tailored pants with a dark grey crew-neck sweater that captured the imprint of his muscles. His black shoes looked as if they had just been shined, and his cologne was breathtaking. This man was dressed, and he was as fine as fine could be. My knees buckled as I looked at him from the bottom of his feet to the top of his head. I took another deep breath.

In my exhale, I called his name, "Gavin."

He didn't waste any time. He lightly brushed his way past me, without asking if it was okay for him to come in. I slowly closed the door. I didn't want to turn around and face this man because I knew the time had come for me to answer for what I did. There was such an uncomfortable silence and I could feel him staring at me from behind.

I turned around and said, "Well, hello, Gavin."

His response was very cold. "Mya."

There I stood in front of the man I'd dated since the tenth grade. We'd gone to every game, dance, movie and prom, and we both graduated with honors. We were part of every debate club in our town. Together, we won more competitions than they could host. Gavin and I made quite a name for ourselves, and we always told each other we were going to be great lawyers.

My life with Gavin couldn't have started any better. Gavin had our whole life planned for us, but he never stopped to consider what I wanted. After we graduated high school, we picked our college classes during the summer, and yes, we both were excited about the life we were building together. Gavin had mapped out our life. We planned to become Mr. and Mrs. Washington after graduation. I couldn't have been happier. I'd loved Gavin ever since that first kiss in his bedroom.

Everything I'd ever experienced was with this man. So, when Gavin proposed to me, I didn't give it a second thought. Of course, I said, "Yes!" This man was everything I could ever want in a man. So why was I so unhappy? We lived in the dorms in our first few years of college. Then, we moved in together to share a studio apartment close to the dorms. I was honored that Gavin wanted to spend the rest of his life with me. On campus, hardly anyone called me Mya. Just like in high school, almost everyone knew and referred to me as Gavin's girl.

Gavin is working toward his dreams. He is sound in *his* identity, but who *am I*? I've started to feel like I have no identity. I have become so conflicted in my spirit because all my dreams have yielded to following Gavin's dreams. Where's my input? If Gavin said, "We're going to do this," we did it. When did it become okay to follow his dreams and not my own? Gavin always knew he was going to be a lawyer. I jumped in on his dream because I liked the whole idea of us being lawyers together, not to mention the prestige that comes along with it.

I had been pulled into Gavin's dreams. I had been living up to what everyone thought Gavin and I were supposed to be. His parents were so proud. Kyle and my grandparents were proud. Gavin was proud. Everyone was proud, except me. Something in me was changing. I wanted my own dreams to come true. But I didn't know how to tell my fiancé that I didn't want his dream anymore.

I was afraid to tell him that I wanted to stand with the elite doctors of the world. I wanted to become an anatomy professor and study the human body. I wanted to discover cures for diseases that there are no cures for yet. I wanted to present my knowledge on The Discovery Channel. But I knew he would laugh at me if I told him. He wouldn't believe in my dreams like I believed in his. Yet, watching him go after his dreams so aggressively, and not letting anything detour him, ignited that same passion within me for my own dreams.

I knew pursuing my dreams would mean I'd have to stand on my own. I couldn't depend on Kyle and Gavin to tell me what to do. Standing alone was a bit scary for me, but my dreams were burning in my soul. I couldn't take hiding behind Gavin and his lawyer idea one more day. I had to break out somehow. I daydreamed of the way I'd stand in front of the camera, what I'd wear, how I'd articulate my thesis and my theories. I thought about how I'd present my hypotheses and speculations.

Gavin never even noticed that I was drifting away from him. That's why I took my beautiful one-and-a-half-carat diamond ring, put it on the pillow, shut the door, and said goodbye to my life with Gavin. I didn't have a plan when I left, and my future was very unclear. But I was hoping to get clarity on who I was—without him. Time seemed to fly by because the semester ended, and I still hadn't made one step toward pursuing my dreams.

Gavin graduated top of his class, just like I knew he would. Now, he stood before me, waiting for an explanation as to why I'd left. When he asked the question, as educated as I am, I gave the dumbest, most-arrogant answer I could give.

I said, "Look how long it took you to come after me."

Gavin didn't hesitate to use his elaborate vocabulary to chop me to pieces. He took this moment to remind me how it isn't every day that people are afforded the opportunity that was afforded to us. He also told me I was throwing my life away. He was starting to sound like he was talking to a troubled teenager. The more Gavin spoke, the angrier I got—until I had to stop him in the middle of his rant.

"I followed my heart. I've moved on and now I have a new man in my life."

I could see the confusion in his eyes. Silence filled the air. It didn't seem like I could say anything right now. He slowly walked over to me as I looked down to avoid eye contact. I don't know what to expect. Inside, I was yelling, *Gavin, I just need to figure some things out!* But my mouth was saying all the wrong things.

Gavin lifted my chin with his index figure and made me look him in the eyes. In a calm, deep voice, he said, "How could you have moved on when you aren't done with me yet?"

I stood there, speechless, looking for a way out of this conversation. I heard the key turn the lock and I thought, *Yes! Thank you, Kyle, for interrupting this conversation I'm not ready to have!* The door opened. I had never been so happy to see Kyle enter a room because Gavin surely was going to make me explain myself. I heard those sweet words Kyle always says once he sees Gavin.

"My man, Gavin!"

They hugged. You could tell Kyle was so proud of his best friend. I stood back, embarrassed. I looked away.

Kyle asked, "Am I interrupting something?"

I quickly responded, "No, you two catch up. I'll talk to you two later."

Gavin put his arms around me, pulled me close, and kissed me partly on my cheek and my lips. Then he said, "This isn't over. We *will* continue our conversation later."

The look in his eyes told me that when we talked again, I would surely answer for my committed sins.

Chapter 7
Mya's Truth

When Gavin said it wasn't over between us, he meant just that. He came over to talk, and I figured I owed him that since I'd walked out on him without an explanation. I wouldn't even take his calls to explain myself. I did everything at Kyle's house. My mail even came there. So, it wasn't abnormal for Gavin to meet me at Kyle's so we could talk.

Gavin always had a way with words. We talked all of five minutes before Gavin made me remember why I fell in love with him. I had no idea why it was so hard for me to tell him I didn't want to follow his dreams anymore. I guess I didn't want to hurt him. As I tried to tell him, I stumbled over my words.

In the middle of me trying to explain why I left, Gavin interrupted, "Mya, stop. Why can't you just say my dreams were not your dreams anymore?"

I thought, *Well, hell. If you knew that, why are you letting me make a fool of myself stumbling over my words?*

Gavin went on to tell me how he'd noticed how detached I was from him. At first, he couldn't put his finger on what was wrong. Since we talked about everything, he figured I would come to him and tell him when I was ready. But that was part of the problem. I took *everything* to him, and he always figured it out for me. I needed to make this decision on my own, *for me.*

Gavin remembered me saying that I wanted to be a professor of anatomy long before we received a full scholarship to the university. I thought it was my destiny to be what Gavin and I loved in high school, but I knew in my heart I wanted something different. I just didn't know how to get it. Kyle and Gavin always carried me, and they were all I had. I didn't know how to break away from that. Gavin told me that he liked it when I became vulnerable with him. I acted so tough sometimes that he didn't get to see that softer side of me. Gavin assured me that he would support my dreams, no matter what they were. He also told me that I made him feel like he had done something wrong. It crushed him to come home and find my ring on his pillow.

Gavin pulled me into him and leaned in to kiss me. I had to stop him.

"Gavin, I have to tell you something."

Gavin replied, "Can't it wait? I miss you."

He pressed his lips against mine. I had always been weak for this man. Who was I trying to fool? This wasn't over. Gavin kissed me all the way to the bedroom. Once he laid me down on the bed, he started from my neck, kissing and licking my body like only he could. As he kissed me, he said, "I'm going to make you have an orgasm for each month you were gone." I left school in December right after winter break and it was now May.

I wasn't sure if I could handle Gavin, but he was doing his thang. When I had that first orgasm, Gavin looked up and said, "That's one." Not long after that, he looked me in the eye again—my body is still trembling—and said, "That's two."

I'd shared everything with this man. He was determined to make sure I never ran away from him again. He took me there again and again. I always said that Gavin must have read my anatomy books because he made my body do everything those books said it could do. Gavin flipped me every way he knew how. Then, he laid me on my back and kissed between my thighs. When his lips touched my lips, my eyes rolled into the back of my head. Gavin was damn good at what he does. He came up for air, looked me in my eyes and lifted my legs gently in the air. I felt his manhood enter my body. My vagina released the rest of the fluids my body had left.

I mumbled softly, "Oh, Gavin! I'm cumming."

Gavin knew that kissing me while I was having an orgasm always made my orgasms harder. So, he stuck his tongue in my mouth and I couldn't stop cumming. I felt Gavin's manhood extend inside me.

"Come out, Gavin."

"I'm not taking it out!"

Gavin released inside me. I could feel his sperm going through my body as we both went to that place of ecstasy together. I came again. I'd never let Kyle put those sheets back on his bed again.

Gavin put his face against mine and whispered softly in my ear, "That's five."

He had surely won this round. As we were lying close to one another, trying to avoid the wet spot in the bed, I told Gavin, "I have something to tell you."

Right after I said that, there was a knock at the door. I tried to ignore it because, on Thursdays, I had a standing lunch date with Stanley. I'd met Stanley about two months ago. Even though we met consistently every Thursday, you would think he would realize that if I didn't answer my phone, I was busy.

Why would he just pop up? I thought.

Trying to act like I didn't hear the door, Gavin said, "You want me to get that?"

"No!" I said in a panic. I rushed to put a robe on. "Wait right here, Gavin, while I get the door."

I hurried to the door, hoping to get rid of Stanley before Gavin saw him. I was unsuccessful. I opened the door and Stanley barged in. He was so happy to see me.

I told him, "I'm tired and haven't showered yet. I'll call you later." I tried to shove him out the door. He wouldn't go for that. As if my luck couldn't get any worse, Gavin came out the bedroom, wearing just his black Calvin Klein boxer briefs. His chest was ripped with his six-pack in full effect, looking like he was modeling for a magazine. I knew this could only get ugly for me.

"Mya, is everything okay?" Gavin asked.

Stanley stopped in his tracks and looked Gavin up and down. "Mya, who is this?"

I had to get a hold of myself. So, I did what any decent woman would do: I introduced them.

"Gavin, this is Stanley. Stanley, this is—"

Stanley interrupted me. "Gavin?"

Stanley knew all about Gavin because I couldn't stop talking about him during our early dating phase. Stanley became enraged. I'd told Stanley it was over between me and Gavin. So, of course, Stanley wanted to know what Gavin was doing standing in front of him in his boxers and no shirt. Stanley had barged in so quickly that I didn't get a chance to close the door behind him all the way. Imagine my surprise when I heard a voice coming from the door.

"Hello? Hello? Hello?"

My back was to the door, but I stopped dead in my tracks. I never turned around because I would know that voice if a symphony was playing in the background and she called my name. My feet were cold and planted on the floor, but I knew I had to think fast. I pushed Gavin toward the back so he could put his clothes on. I hurried to put my skirt and top on, and I run back into the living room. I admit the embarrassment was real. I ran back to the front, barely lifting my head.

"Grandma, where did you come from?"

"No need to send him back there now. I've already seen all that!"

I still couldn't turn around and look my grandmother in the face. But that didn't stop her from getting in my face.

"Well, hello, Mya."

"Grandma, I know this looks really bad—"

"No, Mya. It doesn't look bad. You have one half-naked man, one fully dressed man, and you're half-naked. So, it looks like you were getting ready to have a good time—or you've already had one."

I stood there like I was five years old and I'd just got caught with my hand in the candy jar. Suddenly, this stupid excuse for a man yelled out, "No, she already had a good time, but I wasn't part of it! The door was open because I caught her having sex with her ex, and they probably did it back there in her brother's bed where she had sex with me just the other day!"

My mouth opened so wide that a freight truck could have parked right in it. My grandmother looked puzzled because she knew nothing about Stanley. I stood there, humiliated. I was at a loss for words.

Grandma asked, "Excuse me, but who are you?"

"I'm Stanley and Mya is my girl. I want some answers."

Stanley just stood there, as if he wanted me to choose him over Gavin. He wanted me to look Gavin in the face and declare that I was his woman. My grandmother looked at me with so much confusion.

Out of nowhere, Stanley yelled, "You don't have to choose; I'll choose for you. Man, you can have her!"

Gavin and Stanley got into a yelling match.

Gavin yelled at Stanley, "You can't give him something that's already mine. And if you know what's good for you, you won't ever come back this way again."

I had to stop this before it escalated into a fight between the two of them. I called each of their names, but they ignored me. I jumped in the middle and they shoved me out the way. I had to expose my secret. I knew it probably wasn't the right time, but everything else about me seemed to have been exposed.

"Stanley! Gavin! Both of you please just shut up! Gavin, I've been trying to tell you something!" I paused as water filled my eyes. I knew I was getting ready to break Gavin's heart, but I had to release this secret I was holding. I held my head down and softly said, "Stanley, I'm pregnant." As I raised my head, I looked Stanley in the eyes and say again, "Stanley, I'm pregnant."

It seemed like the whole room shrunk. All the yelling in the room stopped. It was as if the walls caved in on me. Gavin and Grandma stared at me. Gavin had a look of disbelief on his face. I didn't even want to turn around and look at my grandmother. I could just feel her eyes burning the back of my head.

Stanley dropped his head. When he looked up again, he asked, "Who are you pregnant by, Mya? You're sleeping with both of us. So, how do you know whose the father of your baby?"

"How dare you go there with me! I know who the father of this baby is! Why don't you take a moment and remember back about six weeks ago. Yes, that's right! Um...think! Gavin just got home yesterday. Is it sinking in now? Can you add? Do you need assistance in counting?"

Stanley took a step backward. I shamefully glanced over at Gavin, hating to see the hurt look on his face. I could barely look him in his eyes, but I saw the pain on his face. Gavin slowly walked over to me and I quickly looked away. He grabbed my face and made me look him in the eyes.

"You knew you were pregnant, and you had sex with me?"

I had no response as my eyes once again filled with water.

Stanley interrupted and said, "Mya, I have a better question. Did you stop to think about my wife?"

Grandma broke her silence. "Mya, this man is married and you're sleeping with him?!"

Stanley told me he was leaving his wife, but it wasn't that he was leaving his wife *for me*. "Your wife?! You said you were leaving your wife!"

"Well, there's a snowball's chance-in-hell of that happening because she's pregnant, too. My obligation is to my wife, not my mistress."

Stanley took this opportunity to make me feel lower than I've ever felt. He told me, "I'm never leaving my wife for you." To add insult to injury, he took twenty dollars out his pocket, threw it in my face, and said, "This is what I have on your abortion. You better make the rest happen. And don't even think about calling me again!"

I felt like a ton of bricks had fell on me. Gavin jumped up and told Stanley, "It's my nut that's on that baby's head now. I suggest you get the hell out of here! She ain't ever going to want for nothing, and you don't ever have to worry about her phone call again."

I couldn't believe what I was hearing. The worst part of this is that it played out in front of Grandma. Gavin may have been a Yale graduate, but he surely had a little street in him. That was so attractive at the time.

Stanley turned around and stormed out the house. Gavin looked at me and said nothing. He grabbed his things and left. He was too upset for me to run after him, so I just let him go. Kyle always told me never to become a stepmother. I'd not only allowed myself to be treated like one, but I'd become one. Yet again, I knew the day would come when I would have to answer for my committed sins.

Chapter 8
Kyle's Struggle

When I want to think, I go back to the park where Mya and I grew up. I always seem to get answers to my questions or problems when I go there. It's as if my mother speaks to me and always guides to the right things. No matter how much I mask the hurt, I've always struggled with things from my past. I've struggled with my own insecurities of being a man. This day, I was really struggling. I needed to release all the thoughts that were clouding my mind and judgment. I have always looked at men and wondered if I could be bi-sexual. Ever since I was a little boy, I was told, "Be a man. Men don't cry! Men are strong and men take care of business." Sometimes, I feel weak. Sometimes, I feel vulnerable. Sometimes, I want to cry—and all of these are attributes of a woman. When women feel these things, they rely on the comfort of a man. This confuses me because I feel as if I need to rely on the comfort a man, as well. I want to be comforted. I want to be held. Does that make me bi-sexual or does that make me a gay man?

On my way to the park, I called a good friend of mine—Kenny. I met Kenny at the gym in the New Center building in downtown Detroit. Kenny was about five-nine and dark-skinned with a muscular build. He had a vigorous workout plan, which is what attracted me to him. One day, I was watching him work out and I asked him about his routine. Eventually, we exchanged numbers and we met at the gym frequently.

Kenny and I hit it off from the first, "Hello." We started talking outside the gym, which enabled us to learn a whole lot about each other's lives. The closer we got, the deeper the secrets we revealed to each other. Kenny had the neatest dreadlocks I'd ever seen on a man or a woman. There never seemed to be a dreadlock out of place. Kenny was well-educated, holding a master's degree in Engineering. He was also a car designer engineer in the automotive industry.

Kenny had a deep voice and was a very distinguished-looking man. He wasn't a bad-looking woman either. He showed me pictures of him dressed up and I had to take another look. I couldn't tell it was a man. Kenny was a cross-dresser, but he didn't reveal himself as that right away. It wasn't until I revealed my deepest insecurities that he told me about his cross-dressing. We told each other things we never could—or *would*—share with anyone. We figured, if we kept each other's secrets, our friendship would be just fine.

Kenny didn't appear to be a gay man, but I didn't appear to be a man who had gay thoughts either. I thought, with everything I'd shared with Kenny, he would soon make a move on me. I wasn't sure how I was going to respond. *Should I welcome and explore it, or should I take control of my thoughts?* I was totally confused when it came to Kenny because, when he entered the room, his testosterone surely filled the air. His handshake almost broke mine. Looking at him, there was no confusion about him being a man. Parts of me just wanted Kenny to take me in his arms and hold me. I'd been a rock for so many people. When was I going to get a rock?

I was confused as to how this man, who dressed like a woman, provided such a sense of security for me. I had to grab my crotch and deepen my voice just to make sure I was still a man. Kenny was very articulate and very easy to talk to. He always gave me some of the best, sound advice. Most of the time, I couldn't wait until the next time we talked. He was so compassionate, yet stern.

I saw his car coming down the street. Great minds think alike because we both drove the same type of car: a fully loaded 2020 Jaguar. Kenny's car was smoky grey with black leather interior and a dashboard full of gadgets fit for a man. My Jag was eggshell cream with peanut butter interior. We both had tinted windows and sunroofs. By far, we had two of the finest cars on the market.

When Kenny pulled up, I flagged him over to the bench where I was sitting. Normally, we would meet at some bar or restaurant. This was the first time I suggested we meet at the park. I just needed answers. I needed to be completely transparent. This was the only place I could let go and be just that. We greeted each other with a manshake, and right away, Kenny said, "You look different."

He was always so observant. I came right out with it.

"Kenny, I'm struggling with my role as a man."

"Explain to me what you mean by that."

I took him back to me at twelve. "Life forced me to become a man, but my mind is still trapped at twelve years old, in my bedroom. I see my mother, my angel, holding her chest, and I hear Ronald's horrifying voice. It won't let go of me. It's almost as if pieces of me died with her. I'm tired of being a sexually irresponsible man, who's hurting and sleeping with a different woman every other night. I feel like if I told a man to hold me just once, and tell me that he loves me, that would make everything alright. I'm ready to settle down. But ready to settle down to what? Will I be settling down to a life of uncertainty? Will I be settling down to a life of homosexuality? Will I love my wife, but desire a man? I love women, but I want the comfort of a man. So again, what will I be settling down to?"

Kenny listened to me for a good twenty minutes. I told him everything I'd been holding inside of me. When I was done, he asked me, "Have you ever confronted Ronald about the death of your mother? Or the physical and mental abuse he put you through?"

"I hate Ronald so much that confronting him has never crossed my mind. I can't bear to even look at him, let alone confront him."

Kenny explained, "Parents don't think little boys need fathers to hold, hug and kiss them. Little boys need to hear, 'I love you' from their fathers. They need to hear, 'Good job.' They need their father's approval and they need to feel like they made their dad proud. But there are so many fathers in the home and absent. Some are completely absent from the home altogether. Either way, little boys grow up thinking they must become a man's man before their time. So, they become hard and hard to deal with. They continue the cycle with their children. They love on and give affection to their daughters, while they teach their sons to be resentful and uncaring."

Kenny was making a lot of sense, until he started talking about me forgiving Ronald. This was something I'd told myself over and over that I would never do.

But Kenny explained, "Forgiveness may be part of your healing."

"How do you forgive the person who killed your mother?"

"You may need to confront Ronald, forgive him, then forgive yourself. If you don't forgive him, he will control your life for the rest of your life."

I understood everything, except forgiving myself.

"Why should I forgive myself for something that was *done to me*? I just want to forget it all. The abuse, my mother's death, my bedroom."

"Forgiving yourself is simply letting go of what you are holding against yourself. You haven't forgiven yourself because, on some level, you blame yourself for what happened to you. You also need to confront your pain and allow yourself to feel what you feel. But at some point, you have to heal from the pain that has been caused to you."

There was a long pause. I saw a peculiar look on Kenny's face. Kenny broke the silence, "Kyle, do you believe in God?"

I chuckled and asked, "Who?" I took a deep breath and continued. "I used to, but God has never been there for me. So why should I believe in Him?"

"Who do you think brought you this far?"

"Me. I suffered the hurt of losing my mother, growing up in a drug-infested house and being abused. I got blowjobs from women I didn't even know, all while raising my sister on my own. I suffered through that pain. God didn't do that. He didn't suffer for me."

"So, you're saying Jesus didn't suffer?"

"No. I said God didn't suffer. God is a coward. He sent His Son to suffer. What kind of man is that?"

"Wow. Kyle, I have question for you."

"Yeah, man. What's that?"

"Would you let someone hang your son until he dies?"

"Man, what's your point? I didn't come here for a Bible lesson; I can go to church for that."

"Naw. You said God was a coward. The way I see it, you're the coward."

I got very defensive, stood, and said, "What? Man, who are you calling a coward?"

Kenny stood and said, "The same man who just stood up and confronted me is the same man who needs to confront the things he's running from." Kenny and I stood in each other's face, looking each other in the eye. He struck a nerve and so many things ran through my head.

I had to stand down because he was right.

"Kyle, man, I can't explain why God allowed all those things to happen to you. But Jesus made a choice and you have a choice. God didn't force Him to stay on that cross. Nobody's forcing you to stay in your past. If you had God at twelve, you have Him now. You must seek Him. You can blame God all you want. But it's your sins, your poor choices, and your selfishness that prevents you from having a relationship with the Father. God is love. God is forgiveness, and I know you've heard, 'All things work together for good to those who love God, to those who are the called according to His purpose.' You are a part of God's purpose. But it's up to you to figure out what that purpose is. I am a Christian man, and I believe in the death, burial and the resurrection. You died at twelve. You buried yourself all this time. Now it's time for your resurrection."

The look on my face when he said he was "a Christian" told him everything I was thinking. But I still had questions. "Kenny, I don't mean no disrespect, but how are you a Christian man when you're a cross-dresser? Isn't that a sin? Aren't you just as confused as I am?"

"Did you just judge me?"

"No, I'm not judging. I'm asking."

"First, no. I am not confused. I know why I cross-dress, and I am not a gay man. I cross-dress because of my wife."

All this time, I thought Kenny was on the downlow. He wears a wedding ring, but I assumed he was in some type of domestic partnership. But now that I knew he had a wife, I was inquisitive to find out why he cross-dressed *because of her*. I couldn't wrap my mind around it.

"Why do you cross-dress because of your wife?"

"Kyle, everything happens for a reason. There's even a reason you and I met. It's all part of God's plan."

I thought to myself, *I can't take another God talk, story or Scripture. Man, just stop it with the God talk!*

Kenny went on to reveal the most shocking secret about his wife. "My wife is fighting some of the same demons you are."

He paused for a moment. I could tell what he was getting ready to say still affected him, but I wasn't ready for what he would say next.

"My wife's mother started molesting her when she was ten years old. She told her she was preparing her for how to survive in life. She taught her, at ten years old, how to masturbate. She used sex toys on her and made her experience orgasms at this early age. She started letting her boyfriends have sex with her when she turned thirteen.

When she was about nineteen, she started having an affair with her mother's boyfriend. When her mother caught them in bed together, the boyfriend and the mother beat her up so badly that anyone could barely recognize her. Then, they threw her in an alley and left her for dead.

"On that day, I was driving down the street and I saw this woman stumbling from the side of an alley. She stumbled in front of my car and I almost hit her. She was bleeding and weak. They beat her so badly that she barely knew her name. When I jumped out my car to try to help her, I had to convince her I wasn't going to hurt her. After I got her to trust me, I drove her to the hospital and I've never left her side since. I know God sent her to me, and I promised Him I would love, honor, cherish and respect her. Mentally, my wife never recovered from the experiences she went through.

"With everything my wife has been through, I dress up in women's clothing because my wife still longs for the love of her mother, but she needs the strength of a man. I don't understand it because the natural mind would not want to be bothered with a person like her. But my wife is trapped by everything her mother did to her, and she never got closure. That may sound ridiculous to some people, but I do it because I love her. I'm willing to make a damn fool of myself and go against everything I believe as a man to take care of her. I promised God I would love my wife as He loves the church. My wife never got the chance to confront her mother because that same boyfriend who raped my wife, and had an affair with her, ended up killing her mother.

Now, my wife is trapped because she can't confront her past and she doesn't have the answers to why and where her mother's pain stemmed from, which made her do those things to her daughter.

"Kyle, I have never experienced any of the things either of you have. That's why I didn't judge her, and I don't judge you. I can't imagine the things you both have to deal with on a day-to-day basis. That's why I make it a point not to judge things I don't understand. Kyle, I've listened to you and you are not a gay man. I think you're mentally exhausted from running. You never had a father to tell you that he loves you. You never had a father to hug you and you want that. I believe you're exhausted from never being able to release the anger you feel from your mother's passing and having to live with Ronald.

"Even though you love your sister, you're even exhausted from that. You took the abuse to save your sister from experiencing it, trying to keep her out of the hell you were living in. In the process of raising her to be a hell of a woman, no one has told you to look in the mirror and see that you're a hell of a man. Your mother had to be some special type of woman for you to take her principles and values and raise you and sister by them. You're an amazing man, Kyle—a little whorish—but you're a good guy.

"Kyle, you're tired and I think you need to find Ronald. Confront him about your mother's death and confront him about the atrocious life he created for you. Forgive him, forgive yourself and ask God for forgiveness for all the ridiculous anger you have toward Him. Let God in your heart. I'm not talking about religion or attending the local church. I'm talking about the one true God. Then, that dark cloud can be released from over you.

"My wife has cheated on me and it hurts like hell. We still struggle in our marriage to this day. But my prayer every day is to be the best husband I can be for her. My vows said, '...for richer, for poorer, in sickness and health;' that means mental sickness, too. Whatever it is, it's my responsibility to take care of her. I cross-dress in the privacy of our home. I shared it with you because you shared some deep, personal stuff with me. When we are outside the house, and even in our home, she knows I am the man and she is the woman. She never disrespects me. We don't do this every day; we only do it when she needs it. Nobody knows of this sacrifice I make for my wife. But I supply all the love, protection, security, loyalty, conversation, faithfulness, trustworthiness, reliability and dependability my wife needs.

"I don't have any homosexual tendencies. I am purely a heterosexual man. I pray with and for my wife every day, and my faith in God is what's going to deliver her. But He is going to deliver her in His timing, and His timing is not my timing. We all have our secrets. We all have things we don't want anyone to know, and no sin is greater than any other. All of us in this world are one sin short of going to hell. The demons in your mind, my mind, my wife's mind—only God can cast them out. If you keep feeding that negative spirit, it will kill you.

"It takes courage to let go of the things that hurt us. It takes courage to cross-dress for your wife when you know you're a man. I've been telling my wife for years that she must let it go, but she just isn't ready. My wife still cries at night, and sometimes, she wakes up in a cold sweat, thinking she's back on the side of the road, half-naked and lifeless. Every time she wakes up in these cold sweats, I'm there. I hold her while she cries. I comfort her. I protect her and I let her know I will never let anyone hurt her again.

"Kyle, you have to have faith that what's in front of you is greater than what is behind you. If you didn't get it during your childhood, don't mess up and *not get it* in your adulthood. Only you determine what it is. Give it to God. Forgive your stepfather for the things he did and *did not* do. Release yourself from the pain. You know the saying, 'Hurt people hurt people.' I'm sure Ronald has his own story, but I know someone who has the greatest story. God specializes in the things we cannot control or do ourselves. My wife can't deliver herself. That's why I pray for her until God does. You can't deliver yourself; that's why you need to call on the higher power who can—Jesus.

"You already gave your life to Him and He has never left you. You left Him. But, all this time, you've been listening to His voice. That's how you raised your sister the way you did. That's how you became the man you are today, faults and all. And, another thing. God uses whomever He wants to get His message to His people. He can use a drunk, a black man, a white man, a gay man, and yes, a cross-dressing man. Listen to His voice, Kyle. God doesn't take salvation back.

"You're a good man. You raised your sister, graduated high school, put yourself through college, and started your own business. You're raising your son and you aren't even with his mother. You are a great man and you should be proud of that. You must believe in yourself. Only God can give you everything the enemy has stolen from you. All you have to do is surrender. It's not by chance we met; it was by design. God knew what you needed, and He sent me to befriend you. You needed someone you could trust who wouldn't judge you, someone who would understand you. That person is me."

My conversation with Kenny was probably one of the deepest conversations I'd ever had. No one had ever told me to face my fears. No one had ever told me that I was a good man. I didn't even realize what a man looked like until this very moment.

Kenny and I sat in silence for a moment while I pondered the things he'd said to me. I wanted to cry out loud, but I remembered that real men don't cry. I couldn't see myself crying in front of another man, so I held back my tears.

When I looked up, I saw a white Mercedes-Benz pull up behind Kenny's car. Kenny told me that he wanted me to meet his wife. I, too, wanted to meet this woman who he admired so much. He went to the car to greet her, opened her door, and helped her out of her car. I couldn't see her face from the street, but she stood about 5'4" and was light skinned. She wore a red and white dress that accented the curves of her body. I could see her body was very shapely.

As she walked toward me, I noticed that she had thick legs. She didn't have on any stockings and there wasn't a scar on them. This woman didn't have a hair out of place. She looked as if she was coming straight from the beauty salon. As she walked toward me, I thought, *Kenny's wife is fine*.

I was drawn to the chocolate diamond necklace she wore around her neck. The closer she got, the more I recognized this necklace. The necklace had come from my jewelry store. When I looked at her face, I couldn't hide my facial expression.

"Lisa?" I asked, waiting for confirmation.

"Kyle?"

Kenny became very defensive. In his deepest voice, he asked, "How do you know my wife?"

I froze. I couldn't tell Kenny, "Your wife gives me blow jobs and I would have slept with her if my son hadn't busted in on us. Not to mention, I gave her the diamond necklace she's wearing in order to sleep with her."

I knew I had to say something, but Lisa saved both of us. She jumped in and said, "Babe, this is Kyle, my boss."

"How do you two know each other?" she asked.

I looked at Kenny, and again, I didn't dare tell her the complexity of our friendship.

He jumped in before I could speak and said, "I met Kyle at the gym. I left one of my bags, and he was nice enough to meet me here and bring it to me. I wanted you to meet him because he's become a really good friend, but it seems you two already know each other."

The air was very uncomfortable.

Lisa replied, "Well, Kyle. I guess I'll see you at work tomorrow."

She turned to Kenny and gave him a very passionate kiss, while looking at me from the corner of her eye. After they kissed, Lisa said, "Babe, I'll see you at home." She hurried back to her car.

Kenny looked at me, shook his head, and said, "My wife is something else."

"Yes, she is. She's a very good assistant. She really knows the business and she never comes in late."

"You must be a good boss because she never comes home and says, 'I hate my boss.'"

At this point, I was very uncomfortable. All I could think was, *This woman gave me head.*

We shared a laugh and we both said at that same time, "This stays between us."

We laughed again. Kenny and I grabbed hands, gave each other a man hug, and said our goodbyes. I let out a sigh of relief because the last thing I wanted to deal with was Kenny finding out that I'd messed around with his wife.

I turned around and took one last look at the park. I got into my car and drove down the street. The conversation with Kenny played over and over in my head. I heard my mother's voice in my head, as well. My mind was really doing a number on me. I had so many thoughts and feelings running through my mind. Out of nowhere, I heard the song my mother used to sing to me when I was little.

"Yes, Jesus loves me. Yes, Jesus loves me. Yes, Jesus loves me, for the Bible tells me so . . ."

I could hear her voice as if she was in the car with me. Before I knew it, I was humming the words to this song. Then, I started singing the words and the tears fell from my eyes. I wiped my tears away quickly because I was taught as a little boy that you were a weak man if you cried. Crying seemed pointless to me. I knew if I started crying, I'd never stop. I really wanted to cry, but I couldn't. The anger of wanting to cry, and the thought of being a weak man if I cried, infuriated me. So, I started speeding. I would rather drive my car into a wall than to allow myself to cry as a grown man.

I would not cry. I was angry, bitter and hurt. I would never forgive him. My perception of life had been totally altered. I was tired, confused and perplexed. I was at a complete loss regarding where my life was supposed to be.

And, still, I refused to cry.

Chapter 9
Kyle and Ronald

I was so full of rage. I was driving so fast it's no wonder the police didn't pull me over and give me a ticket. I stormed into my house, full of emotions when the worst thing that could happen happened.

In my living room sat Grandma, Mya and Ronald. I saw a look of somberness on everyone's face. I automatically thought something had happened to Grandpa. The air was so thick that I knew something was surely wrong. Before I grabbed Ronald by his shirt and killed him right where he stood, I asked Grandma, "What's wrong?" Mya had tears in her eyes. Grandma took me by my hand and told me to have a seat. Grandma looked into my eyes and her eyes were glassy.

I didn't know what to expect. I was confused because Ronald was sitting in my living room. All I could think about was how now was the time to confront him. But my mind was set on finding out what was wrong with Grandpa. "Grandma, just tell me what's wrong."

Grandma says, "Ronald has been diagnosed with cancer and the doctors have given him four months to live."

I paused for a few minutes. Then, I said to myself, *Today is the day I will confront this demon from my past.*

When Ronald and my mother were dating, I'd always felt there was something about him that was very unsettling.

But my mother loved him. So, I tried to love him because she did. After my mother married Ronald, I noticed that he became possessive over her. It was as if he wanted me to disappear. After Mya was born, I really felt like he wanted it to be just my mother, Mya and him. Ronald hated me and he hated the love my mother poured into me.

After Grandma told me that Ronald was dying, I chuckled a little and grinned. Grandma had a look of concern on her face because I didn't look, feel or act concerned. Ronald got up and started walking toward the door. I jumped in front of him, stopping him from leaving.

I looked him straight in his eyes and said, "Oh no, devil. I will release you today."

Ronald knew I was getting ready to expose him. I knew if I didn't release this hatred, I would be trapped in it for the rest of my life. I finally had the opportunity to confront the man who took so much away from me.

"Ronald, you don't get to run anymore. You will hear me out today. My memories with you are so painful that I've tried to eradicate every thought of you from my mind, but the pain I've felt has never gone away."

Grandma stood up. I said, "Grandma, please don't stop me. You're not going to want to hear this, but you have to hear it."

I turned back to Ronald and continued. "I grew up feeling disgraceful, no good, shameful, valueless and vile. You killed me that night in my bedroom, right along with my mother. You desecrated my state of mind, totally obliterating my innocent way of thinking. I lost hope in God, prayer, love and myself.

"I was twelve years old when I was left to raise my sister. I didn't even know who I was. My mother died of a heart attack because her heart couldn't take walking into my bedroom and seeing her husband raping her son. You made us live in a house full of drugs and debauchery. I had to sleep on the floor next to my little sister's bed to make sure you and no one else touched, raped, sodomized, sexually abused, violated, exploited or exposed her to any form of molestation, like you imposed on me. I had to protect her from *you*.

"You were a bi-sexual man before you met my mother. You kept up the appearance of a straight man and carried out your sexual fantasies on me. The women and men you made us live with were all trash. I received a blowjob at the age of thirteen from a woman you allowed into our home. But tell Grandma and Mya who gave me my first one! I was so terrified of you and too ashamed and embarrassed to tell anyone. So, I took it. In my mind, I thought I was strong enough to handle it. As long as you were doing it to me, you wouldn't touch Mya. I've had to battle homosexual thoughts. I've had to battle being a man, a father, a husband and a brother. I've put on an act for so long that I now have no idea where my place is a man in this world.

"I've created fantasies with over two hundred women, trying to prove to myself that I'm not a gay man. I have a son who I must fight for every day to make sure this vicious cycle is broken. I hope every day that I'm man enough for him. And you have the nerve to come in here and lie to us!

"Grandma, this piece of shit isn't dying of cancer! He's dying because the HIV virus he was carrying has turned into full-blown AIDS. I know this because he infected me with the virus. So, Ronald, tell me how does it feel to know that I let you suffer? I got the money and doctors that could have treated you, but I hate you that much. I receive treatment from the best doctors and I'm on the best medication that money can buy. I've already died once. I'm just waiting to see you die. Now tell me, Grandma, who's supposed to forgive who?"

Chapter 10
Mya

Shattered into pieces beyond repair, I hadn't stopped crying since Kyle revealed why he held all that anger, bitterness and hatred buried inside him. I had no idea Kyle had endured so much from my father. I finally understood what happened that night Mama died, but I was so angry with Kyle. We'd shared everything, but this. Kyle and I didn't have any secrets. I thought I knew everything about my brother. How could I be in the same house and not know my brother was being raped? How could I be so close to my brother and not know the anguish he lived in? Kyle made our life look picture perfect, and it was far from it. Kyle used to guard the bathroom door and my room like he was The National Guard.

It seemed as though life had simply become too hard to even have a conversation. As I stared at the four walls, in my mind, they were closing in on me. I was still crying. My mind drifted back to being a little girl, helping my mother wash dinner dishes and listening to her yell at Kyle to get his school clothes ready for the next day. That was when life made sense. I couldn't help but to think that, if my mother were here, none of those things would have happened to Kyle. Then again, that was the reason she lost her life. *God, where are you? Kyle used to tell me you had other kids to look after, but there were two kids over here who have been torn to shreds. You've done nothing to help us.*

I now understand why Kyle hated my father all those years. Kyle had sacrificed so much for me. With all he'd done for me, I had become a disappointment to him. I quit law school just before graduation. I walked out on my fiancé, and now, I'd got myself pregnant by a married man. Kyle tried to protect me from becoming a stepmother, yet I was so close to being one.

It all made sense now. Kyle never wanted me to experience any of the things he experienced. He only wanted me to be with Gavin because he knew Gavin would treat me better than any man I could ever run across. Kyle always wanted what was best for me. Yes, Kyle was way overprotective at times, but I wish I had understood all the things he was trying to get me to understand before I made a mess of my life.

God gave Kyle wisdom beyond his years. At the age of twelve, who would have known how to map a plan out, not just for himself, but for his baby sister, as well? I wished Mama could see him now. She would have been so proud of him. There I was, balled up in this chair with tears streaming down my face. I start singing my Sunday school song.

I remember being a little girl in church. I wore a pink dress, white lace-ruffled socks, white patent-leather shoes, and four ponytails when I sang in the children's church choir. I watched my mother direct as we sang *Nothing but The Blood of Jesus*. As the tears flowed from my eyes, I repeated that chorus again.

I didn't realize that the door had opened, but I felt a presence. Then, I heard a voice.

"You haven't done anything you can't be forgiven for."

I looked up and there was Gavin, standing there for me in my time of need. I called him and he came running. Gavin wrapped his arms around me and let me cry until no more water could come out of my eyes. He took his finger, lifted my chin, and said, "No matter how this baby was conceived, you have a miracle growing inside you. You cannot undo what God has done."

"How do you know I haven't already done it?"

"Because you would have called me from home, not the abortion clinic. Mya, let's go home and figure this out."

I didn't think there was anything to talk about. I didn't want this baby. The best thing to do was to get rid of it. The door opened and the nurse's assistant called my name, "Mya Johnson."

Gavin and I stood together. With tears in my eyes, I looked at Gavin's face, then at the woman standing in the doorway who was waiting for me. I was paralyzed. She called my name again.

"Mya Johnson."

Lady, I'm standing right here! You see I'm the only one in the lobby, so you know I'm Mya Johnson. Can you just wait a damn minute? This is a life-altering decision! I thought.

Gavin said, "Mya, you can't keep running from your mistakes. Please don't do this. We can face this together. Stop adding to the hurt and pain you've already experienced."

I couldn't believe God would allow a man to love me the way Gavin does, especially after all I'd done. I didn't deserve to be loved like this. I knew now that this was the kind of love and the type of man Kyle wanted me to experience.

I looked at Gavin and said, "I'm sorry. I have to do what's best for me."

I walked toward the door and make it halfway through before I heard Gavin yell, "Mya, you can't keep walking out of my life! I love you, and I'll love that baby like it's my very own."

I stopped and turned around. I saw the pain on Gavin's face as the tears rolled from his eyes and mine.

"Don't do it!" he said.

I let that door close behind me, determined to do what I had come to do—get rid of the baby. The nurse took me into a room in the back of the building. As I entered the room, I saw a table with white tissue paper and gray stirrups at the end of the table. She handed me a gown and told me to undress from the waist down and lie on the table.

"The doctor will be right in," she told me.

The room was cold. Tears streamed from my eyes. I got undressed, laid back on the table, and put my legs in the stirrups. The room was silent. As I looked in the corner, I saw what I believed to be a vision. My mother was standing there. This vision seemed so real that I yelled, "Mom!" I couldn't stop the tears from falling. Then, I heard my mother's voice.

"Yes, Jesus loves me. Yes, Jesus loves me. Yes, Jesus loves me for the Bible tells me so . . ."

She used to sing this song to me while I took baths, on the way to school, and when she put me to bed. The song got louder and louder in my head. Then, I heard two knocks on the door and the song stopped.

The door opened slowly. I saw the doctor's white lab coat as he entered the room. The nurse followed behind him. He called my name just to make sure I was the right patient. He pulled the round stool from the corner of the room, not saying a word to me. The nurse laid me back on the bed. The doctor opened my legs, went under the sheet, stuck his fingers into my vagina, and pressed on my stomach. I could see the nurse lubricating the speculum for the doctor. She handed it to him. He inserted it in my vagina, and I heard a clicking noise.

Then I heard, *Yes, Jesus loves me. Yes, Jesus loves me. Yes, Jesus loves me* . . .

Tears streamed down my face as the doctor turned the machine on. He came closer to me and told me to relax. I gasped for air and let out a loud cry.

The nurse said, "Doctor, wait."

My mother's voice was still singing in my head.

I looked at the nurse and said, "I don't want to have an abortion."

The doctor immediately shut the machine off, took the utensil out of my vagina, and left the room. The nurse handed me a washcloth to clean myself up. She looked at me and said, "That guy you left in the waiting room is still waiting for you."

I hurried to put my clothes on and ran down the hall. I flew through the doors. I didn't even care about getting my money back. When I came through those doors, Gavin stood up and I ran into his arms.

"I couldn't do it! I couldn't do it!"

Gavin held me tightly as the tears streamed down both our faces. We left there and went to my apartment. I took a hot bath and lied down on the bed. Gavin put his arms around me, stroked my hair, and held me as I cried. I cried for my brother's hurt. I cried for my mother not being there. I cried for my dying father. I cried for my grandmother's broken heart. And I cried for my unborn child. Life had hit me and all I can do was cry.

Gavin laid his hands on me and said, "Heal her broken spirit, in the name of Jesus."

It had been a long time since I'd had someone lay hands on me and pray.

"Please, Jesus, fix it."

Chapter 11
Kyle Sr. and Kyle Jr.

I finally said it out loud. I was raped. I am a victim of child molestation, physical, emotional and mental abuse. Those were the *spirits in my bedroom*, and this was not an easy confession. I was a prisoner, trapped in my own mind and bound by my past. Everything I was taught to believe as a little boy was distorted. Even though I had a son, family and friends, even with all the years that had gone by, I was still a prisoner.

I left work early and drove around in a daze for hours, just burning gas. Grandma was still at my house, so I didn't want to go home. I didn't feel much like talking. Even though Mya never knew how much I needed her to make it through, I didn't want to discuss anything right now. Mya was the reason I'd survived it all. My mother always told me to take care of my sister. When she died, I made sure I did just what my mother said. That's why I always needed her at my house and I never sent her away, even though she had her own place. I needed Mya to be wherever I was.

When I looked up, I was sitting in front of Naomi's house. I've never just popped up at her house before. But since I was there, I wanted to see my son. Naomi was renting a big, beautiful house in the suburbs. She lived in a working-class neighborhood and the people on her block were nice. I sat outside for a few moments, just to collect myself. I finally got out and rang the doorbell.

I saw Naomi look out the window. She rushed to open the door. She immediately felt something was wrong. As hard as I tried to hide it, she could see the distress on my face. She invited me in. I was immediately greeted by my little man, Kyle Jr. He ran and jumped into my arms, as if he hadn't seen me in months. It made me feel good that he was so happy to see me.

I hugged him tightly as the tears streamed down my face. I held onto my little boy for dear life. Naomi stood off to the side because she knew something was wrong. When I finally put my son down, I wiped my face.

Kyle Jr. asked, "Daddy, what's wrong?"

"I'm just happy to see you."

Kyle Jr. wanted me to play the new game his mother bought him. We played for about half an hour. Then Naomi told Kyle Jr. to get his bath and to get ready for bed, just like my mother used to tell me. I kissed my little man and told him I'd be sure to tuck him in.

When Kyle Jr. went to his room, I fell into Naomi's arms. She held me as if it didn't even matter that I'd broken her heart. She didn't rush me into telling her what was wrong. We sat in silence until I wanted to talk. I didn't hold back anything. I told Naomi everything that had happened from my twelfth birthday party up until that very moment. We talked for two hours.

Some things were difficult to get out. But when I teared up, Naomi held me and squeezed me tighter. I regretted ever hurting this woman. Naomi was truly my one and only love, and I'd really hurt her. She cried with me and let me know that everything was going to be alright. The most difficult part of the conversation was telling her about the HIV virus. We discussed it in its entirety. She agreed to make an appointment with my specialist to be tested. My next appointment was coming up and I wanted to make sure that I was right there for her for her appointment. Since learning about my status, I'd never slept with a woman without a condom.

Naomi cried in my arms. I sincerely apologized for everything I'd put her through. I just hoped that she could find it in her heart to forgive me. She was a good girl, and she let me know that she'd never stopped praying for me. I wasn't ready to have another conversation about prayer, God or anything similar.

Naomi grabbed my hand and said, "Let me show you something."

She took me into a closet where she had labels, sticky notes and letters everywhere, just like a movie. I saw my name throughout this closet. She showed me Kyle Jr.'s side of the closet, which caused me to become overwhelmed with emotion again.

Naomi said, "God always told me to give it time and it would all make sense. I didn't know what you were going through or even had been through. But I did know whatever it was, it would eventually come to pass."

It's funny that when I stopped believing and praying, God had people believing and praying for me. Parts of my conversation with Kenny ran through my mind. My mother's voice ran through my mind. I looked at the wall where my eight-year-old son had been praying for me. All this time, I'd prided myself on being such a big man. But a man teaches his son about God and how to pray. I was so angry with myself because I'd put God in the back of my mind. When I looked at this wall, I knew this was the reason my suicide attempt wasn't successful. This was the reason why I didn't die in my depression. Just maybe, God had brought me through this horrible ordeal because I had a purpose. Maybe God had a plan for me. Being in this room, I couldn't help but to humble myself. Overwhelmed by it all, I fell to my knees.

As a man, I wasn't supposed to cry. But I felt like my breaking point had come. I cried out as a man for the first time. For the first time in my life, I said out loud, "God, I need you!" I couldn't believe it. I was in this closet, calling on the name of Jesus. Crying as a man. Praying as a man. Asking God for help, direction, guidance, love, joy, peace and forgiveness. The tears continued to flow. I hoped my mother was proud of me.

"Lord, break the strongholds in my life, and please give me clarity. I surrender. I surrender my life to you."

I prayed and cried. I prayed and cried some more. I prayed and cried so hard that I must have fallen asleep. When I woke up, the door was shut, and I was alone. Naomi left me to face my demons by myself. This time, I was in a room all by myself and I wasn't afraid. Looking across at me, I saw little Kyle filled with the presence of God.

I asked, "Where have you been?? He reached his arms out to embrace me. I opened my arms. In that moment, a little boy set this grown man free.

I opened the door and the house was quiet. It was about 4 a.m. I looked into Kyle Jr.'s room to see both Naomi and Kyle sleeping. Kyle Jr. was lying in his mother's arms. I didn't want to wake them, so I turned quietly and walked away. As I walked through the kitchen, a small light lit up the countertop. On the countertop was a white envelope. On the front of the envelope was the word, "Dad." My son always wrote me letters. I figured he'd left this letter for me. I took the envelope, turned the light off, made sure Naomi's house was locked up and left.

I started my car and opened the letter.

To my Daddy,

You're the greatest daddy in the world. I love you so much and bunch. You buy me things, you give me wet kisses that I always wipe off, and you're always there to help me. I asked God to protect my whole family, you, Mommy, Auntie Mya, great-grandma, great-grandpa, Uncle Gavin, and Granddad Ronald. God, I love my mommy and daddy. But God, can you make the devil leave my family alone? I love you, Daddy! Amen!

Your #1 fan, Kyle Jr.

I could barely finish the letter as the tears streamed down my face. When Naomi told Kyle Jr. to go into his room, he went in his room. I believe he was listening to every word Naomi and I said. I had had enough emotion for one day. I couldn't cry anymore, but I was feeling something I hadn't felt in a long time. I had a greater sense of self-worth and I knew I could face whatever came my way. I embraced my past and my present. Now, I'd embrace my future.

I drove home with the radio off and I shut my phone off. I just wanted to be in complete silence. When I got home, I stuck my key in the door, dropped my keys on the table, quietly lied down on the sofa, and fell asleep in my clothes.

Chapter 12
Grandma and Mya

I could hear Grandma with her gospel music playing as I stepped onto the porch. Shirley Caesar was one of my grandmother's favorite artists. When she put on Pastor Caesar, she meant business. My mother used to play gospel music and walk the floors at night. I grew up listening to that good old gospel music—Thomas Whitfield, Shirley Caesar, Albertina Walker, James Cleveland and others could be heard throughout the house. I'm not sure when God became a non-factor in my life. But surely, at some point, I stopped believing in Him. Kyle and I both were taught about God. We were taught to pray. One day, we just stopped. We didn't pray anymore. I'm sure Mama turned over in her grave about that.

I stood on the porch and glanced through the window. Sure enough, Grandma was walking the floors and singing. I started to turn around and go to my own house, but I knew I'd have to face Grandma—today, tomorrow or next week. It didn't matter. I knew I was going to have to face her eventually. I put my key in the door and turned the lock. As I entered, Grandma looked up at me. I walked through the door.

"Hey, Grandma," I said in my little girl's voice. I always used this voice when I spoke to my grandmother. I was looking for that Grandma comfort only she could give. I wanted that Grandma hug, that feeling of a grandmother's love that makes you feel like, despite all your mistakes, it's okay.

When we were kids, and we messed up, Grandma gave us the biggest kiss on the forehead. Her exact words were, "Go and sin no more." My mother would get so mad at my grandmother because she always got us out of trouble.

Instead, I got a tone from my grandmother that was dry as the desert heat. When she said my name, it sounded as if I was her biggest disappointment.

"Mya."

I thought, *I really don't want to deal with Grandma right now, and where is Kyle when I need him?*

She walked over to the sofa table where her iPhone was playing and shut it off. I attempted to walk past her and go to my room when I heard my grandmother say, "Little girl, don't you walk away from me!"

I stopped in my tracks. I knew it was getting ready to go down. The only time Grandma used the words "little girl" with me was when she was furious. By the tone of her voice, and the use of her words, I knew I had to tread lightly. I had a lot of respect for my grandmother and she was surely no one to play with.

She turned away from the sofa table and said, "Sit down."

I didn't move. Grandma looked me right in my eyes and asked, "Do I need to repeat myself?"

At that point, I couldn't sit down fast enough. My mother used to ask us, "Do you want me to repeat myself?" That meant you better move and move super-fast into whatever you were being told or asked to do. So, I moved quickly to sit down. I made sure my body language didn't get smart with Grandma because Grandma could read body language well. I knew she wouldn't hesitate to slap me across the face.

After I sat down, Grandma wasted no time with the small talk. She jumped right in. "So, you had an abortion?"

I couldn't believe Grandma started with me this way. My eyes got so big and I knew I was sitting there with the dumbest look on my face. I thought, *How did she know I was contemplating having an abortion?*

Before I could say anything, Grandma said, "Close your mouth. I know you're surprised I know."

I thought, *Did Gavin tell my grandmother on me?*

Grandma quickly said, "You see, I know how you little girls think."

I was trying not to let Grandma see me thinking, but I was surely thinking, *If you call me 'little girl' one more time...*

Grandma knew when and how she said, "little girl," it was very demeaning. It made me feel so small and she knew it. Grandma went on and on, giving her prolific dissertation about how she felt about abortion. If that wasn't enough, she hit me with, "So you were also dating a married man? Tell me something, Mya. When he screwed you, then went home and screwed his wife, who was he cheating on? You or his wife?"

I couldn't believe this came out my grandmother's mouth. She told me how I had reduced myself to being nothing but a piece of ass to a man who had little or no respect for commitment, his marriage, his wife, me, himself, and last, but definitely not least, for God. "A God-fearing man wouldn't run around town on his wife!"

When I thought Grandma couldn't go any lower, she went there.

"So, tell me, Mya, how does his wife taste? Because every time you kissed that man, you were kissing his wife. I'm sure he kisses her every day when he walks out that house!"

Tears streamed down my face. I was trying to control my emotions because this woman was still my grandmother. I sat there with a still face, trying not to have a response one way or the other. But she wouldn't stop.

"You've got a man, but that's obviously not good enough for you because you had to go to bed with someone else's man. And, if that wasn't bad enough—you carrying on like this *wife's* man is your man. Then, you get pregnant by this *wife's* husband. You see where I'm going? She's the *wife*; you're the *other woman*. I can't believe, as intelligent as you are, that you're so stupid to believe he was really going to leave his *wife* for you. Newsflash, little girl: They never leave *the wife* for *the mistress*. They tell you what you want to hear so you will do all the freaky stuff their *wife* has stopped doing because life takes over. Situations happen and they come looking for little girls like you who will lick and suck them until they're satisfied. That's all you were—pure satisfaction for the time being because he never had any intention of leaving his *wife*.

"You had your own fiancé, a man who was prepared to make you a *wife*. But *you* jumped into something and didn't end the relationship you were in. To add insult to injury, you're so irresponsible, negligent, immature and careless that you got pregnant by this *wife's* husband and decided to have an abortion so you wouldn't have to live with the embarrassment and the shame of having this *wife's* husband's child, bringing it into the world as a bastard.

"Now, this man has gone back home to his *wife* and I guarantee you his *wife* won't know anything about you, unless you go knocking on that woman's door, crying the blues about sleeping with her husband, when you have your own single man. Now tell me, why would you mess with a married man?"

As much as I didn't want to cry, Grandma's words hurt me so badly that the tears rolled down my face. Grandma's attack on me was so vicious. You would have thought I slept with her husband. The more she talked, the worse I felt. I already had my own emotions to deal with, without Grandma adding her emotions to my situation and making me feel like I wasn't worth the air I was breathing.

If this had been Kyle, she would have never talked to him like this. If Kyle had been dating a married woman, I'm sure this conversation would have been totally different. If he was here, he wouldn't dare have let Grandma talk to me like this. I wasn't going to listen to another word because everything coming out her mouth was mean and cutthroat. I had to take my dignity back, so I interrupted her.

"Grandma, may I speak?"

"What do you have to say for yourself?"

I knew anything I had to say from this point had to be said without any fear. If I showed fear, she would eat me alive. So, I stood up, boldly looked my grandmother in the face, and replied.

"At the age of ten, my life was turned upside down. I used to watch my father beat my mother senseless, and you knew nothing about that because we weren't allowed to discuss it. I busted in on what would be their last fight, and I watched as my father threw my mother up against a wall. The last visual I have of my mother is her holding her chest and gasping for air.

"I grew up in a drug-infested sex house, where I was offered drugs and sex with men, women and even *my own father*. I was asked to do cocaine with my father. I got my period at age fourteen, and my brother had to wrap me up in a freaking towel because I thought I was dying. I had to rely on books and other people to teach me what my period was.

"I graduated top of my class with honors. I won twelve—twelve—count them—championships from the American National Debate Team. I made the honor roll eleven of the twelve years I was in school. I don't remember seeing you at *any* of those award ceremonies. I received a full-ride scholarship to one of the most prestigious universities based on my character, my strengths, my intelligence and my hard work.

"I had my first sexual encounter one week after I graduated high school and was engaged to that man who I gave my virginity to. I'm twenty-five years old and I've had two sexual partners in my life. I am not a whore, a hoe, or a piece of ass, like you've deemed me to be. I knew what I was doing and how I was doing it. How do you know he wasn't just a piece of wet ass for me?

"I dropped out of law school in my last semester because I was having an identity crisis from trying to fit into my mother's, my brother's, my fiancé's, and my grandmother's Christian world. My brother raised me, and I always did what he said—so much so that I ended up following someone else's dreams, leaving my dreams by the wayside. I have a dream of being an anatomist. My dreams are to receive my doctorate in anatomy, be a professor of anatomy, and travel the world. I will be on television, making new discoveries, come up with different cures for the human body, and make a difference in the world.

"And, yes, I had an affair with a married man. Yes, I got pregnant by a married man. Yes, abortion was the first thing that came to my mind. And, yes, I even went to the abortion clinic. But, you were here stewing in your anger, contemplating how you were going to tear me down just to show me the error of my ways, instead of praying for me like the woman of God you have claimed to be all these years. When you had the chance to show grace and mercy, you blew it.

"I remember when my mother used to walk the floors. She would be praying and when she would come into my room, I would pretend I was sleep. I would peek out from under the covers and watch her stand over me and pray. When she left the room, I would say, 'In Jesus' name,' just as I was taught. Fifteen years later, I'm still riding on the prayers of my mother because I don't even pray for myself. *But* all my mother's prayers met me at my lowest point in life and carried me into making the right decision.

"I remember my mother praying to God, asking Him to show up in my life when I lost my way. Well, God sure does answer prayer because, when I least expected it, I heard her singing that song. I tried ignoring it and moving forward with the abortion anyway. But her voice got stronger and stronger. Those prayers rose in me and reminded me that Jesus still loves me, even though I've made a mistake. Who would have known my mother's prayers would follow me and prevent me from making a bad situation worse?

"I stood here and listened to you rip me apart. And it hurts like hell because you didn't believe enough in prayer that God would change my mind. If you had been praying like Mama, you would have known that God blocked it. I wasn't expecting you to be happy about what I did. Hell, I'm not happy about what I did. But I wasn't expecting you to make me feel worthless. I didn't have the abortion!

"Mama always told me that, one day, I was going to understand the words of the songs we were taught, and I would feel God's presence for myself. Well, Grandma, I got my feeling. I felt His presence and I will be forever changed because of it. Please don't judge me. I made a mistake. Remember, you told me, 'It isn't about how you hard you fall. It's all about what you do when you get up.' I got up, Grandma, and I'm standing tall."

By this time, tears were rolling down her face. When I was done, I thought surely that I was getting ready to bust hell wide open because of the way I spoke to Grandma. I stood and waited. I just knew Grandma was going to slap me to the floor. I was willing to take that slap because I'd finally stood up for myself. I had no idea Kyle was home. But when I looked across the room, Kyle was standing there with such a proud look on his face. He'd heard the whole thing. Kyle knew I'd never stood up for myself. I realized it was time I become a woman with a plan for my life.

Grandma extended her arms, wrapped them around me and said, "Little girl, I love you."

This time when she said, "Little girl," it was different. This time it meant, "I'm still Grandma and you will always be my little girl." She kissed me on the forehead and said, "Go and sin no more."

I now understood exactly what this meant. I understood who God really was. I knew I was going to win.

I had to start over. I prayed, "Lord, I need you in order to win. I ask that you please forgive me for my sins. Amen."

Chapter 13
Mya

Grandma stayed with us another week. We loved having her there because she was a lot of fun when she wasn't angry. Before she left, Kyle wanted to do something special for her as he always did when she came to visit. My brother was the king of nice gifts and making a woman feel as if she was the only woman in the world. That's why he had so many women falling at his feet. If our mother had been alive, between Kyle and me, she wouldn't have wanted for anything.

Kyle decided to take Grandma and me to The Opera House on Saturday night. He purchased tickets to a show called *Common Ground*. *Common Ground* was a dance piece created by choreographer Edgar Zendejas. This piece brought three diverse dance companies together for a classical and contemporarily stunning original piece. Grandma loved dancing. She was a dance instructor for thirteen years, until she couldn't dance any longer. Kyle had also reserved a table at Iridescence, one of his favorite restaurants. Iridescence was a five-star restaurant, located downtown on the sixteenth floor of the Motor City Casino Hotel, which was about ten minutes from The Opera House. I was looking forward to our outing.

Going out with my brother was always an experience because he liked nothing but the best. He always went over and beyond when he went out. Besides, I loved putting on an evening gown and being out on the town. Kyle had something special scheduled for Grandma all week. His plan was to completely make Grandma over. He first sent her to the day spa for a full day of pampering. She got a facial and a full-body massage, along with a mud bath, pedicure and manicure. By the time I picked Grandma up, she was so relaxed that all she wanted to do was go to sleep.

The next day, Kyle took Grandma shopping. I tagged along for the excitement of watching Kyle buy her everything she wanted. I also wanted to help Kyle pick out Grandma's gown for our night out. We had so many bags that we had to go back to the car to drop them off.

Finally, we started shopping for what we had gone shopping for in the first place: Grandma's gown for Saturday. We decided to go to look in some of the boutiques. While in this one boutique, the clerk who was helping us was so busy flirting with Kyle that I thought she was bringing us all the ugly gowns on purpose just to keep flirting. Then Kyle spotted this one gown. When he pointed it out, it was the most beautiful gown in the boutique. We showed it to Grandma, and she loved it. We had her go into the dressing room to try it on. When Grandma came out, the whole store stopped and looked.

The dress was beautiful. It was a single-strap, champagne-colored evening gown with a half-cape on the shoulder of the strap that hung with the beauty of the dress. If there was a little chill in the room, you could also use it as a covering for your shoulders. There was a metallic-gold accent belt around the waist, and it shimmered with small metallic accents.

Grandma looked in the mirror and smiled from ear to ear. The dress was long and form-fitting, and it showed that Grandma still had her flat stomach. This dress accented her curves and the material clung just right, fitting her perfectly.

When Kyle turned around, his mouth dropped. Kyle didn't care who he flirted with. Jokingly, he said, "Oooo, Grandma! If we weren't related, and I saw you out somewhere, I would take you home and let you experience Kyle's love experience."

Grandma blushed. To our surprise, Grandma said, "Boy, Grandma's got a love experience of her own, and a youngster like you couldn't even keep up."

Kyle responded, "Grandma, that's just nasty."

I went to the other side of the store to find Grandma the right undergarments to go with the dress. When I came back, Kyle and Grandma were in line.

When I tried to hand Kyle the undergarments, he asked, "What's this?"

"Kyle, you have to buy the right bra and panties. You've got to make sure Grandma's girls are standing up."

I had never seen Kyle so embarrassed. He said, "I draw the line when I have to see my grandma's underwear. I do not want to know what undergarments my grandmother is wearing." We laughed so hard.

Grandma chimed in and said, "What about Kyle's love experience?"

Kyle replied, "Grandma, I am not looking at your underwear! Here's my credit card. I'll meet you guys outside."

We paid for the items and headed to Nordstrom's to find shoes to match the dress. When we walked in the store, I immediately spotted a pair of shoes that looked like they'd match the dress perfectly. They were a Jimmy Choo closed-toe gold pump, with a three-inch heel. They had the same gold color as the accented belt on the dress. Then, Kyle spotted a soft-gold Christian Louboutin red-bottom shoe. Of course, the shoe Kyle picked out went better with the dress than the shoe I'd picked out. Grandma loved Kyle's shoe. He purchased the shoes and we left the mall.

Grandma was getting tired. Kyle said, "Grandma, we have one more stop, and we'll get takeout and go home."

We pulled up at Kyle's jewelry store. Kyle's jewelry store sold exclusive, expensive jewelry. His jewelry store had an armed guard, as well as a great security system. The choice pieces were kept in a vault and the most expensive pieces were imported upon ordering. The average-priced jewelry was in the display cases. Just in case anyone ever tried to rob the place, the thieves would think they were getting expensive pieces, but they'd really get a lower-class flawed diamond. Kyle sold nothing but diamonds and he'd never had an issue at his store. When the stars came to Detroit looking for jewelry, they all came to Kyle's store. He rented pieces for videos, and his jewelry collection was also online. Kyle was a successful, well-known man. His jewelry store sat in downtown Birmingham, a suburb of Detroit, right on the corner of all the main attractions.

When we arrived, Kyle told Grandma to pick out anything she wanted.

Grandma told Kyle, "You've already spent so much money on me, baby. This is enough."

Kyle replied, "Grandma, please don't worry about the money. I never got a chance to do these things for my mother, so please let me do this for you."

Grandma looked at Kyle, then looked at me with such a proud look on her face. "Your mother would be so happy."

Kyle turned to go to his office. He told his staff, "Make sure my grandmother gets something nice."

Lisa, Kyle's assistant, showed Grandma a few pieces of jewelry. She absolutely fell in love with the pieces. She thought the price was $1600, but it was a $16,000 diamond necklace and earring set. It looked simple, but when the light hit the necklace, you could see the clarity of the diamonds.

Kyle came down with a display of chocolate diamond sets and asked, "Grandma, do you like this?"

"Yes, baby! I love it."

Kyle told his staff to gift-wrap both sets and add the insurance. The sets totaled $22,000. But Grandma looked unhappy.

"What's wrong, Grandma?" Kyle asked, puzzled.

"Baby, I really appreciate it, but I can't accept this."

"Why not, Grandma?"

"Listen, baby. I can't take something like this back home. How do you think it will make your grandfather feel? He can't afford to buy me this type of expensive jewelry."

"Grandma, pick him out something, too."

"Baby, you're missing my point. We live a modest life. And yes, your grandfather buys me very nice things. But $22,000 worth of diamond necklaces and earrings? He can't afford that, so I won't disrespect him and bring it into our house. The dress and shoes, he buys me those things already. So those things won't be offensive to him. But $22,000 worth of diamonds, coming from another man— even if he is my grandson—that would be offensive to my husband."

"I never thought about it like that. I understand, Grandma."

Kyle and I had just learned a life lesson from my grandmother: Never allow any man to outdo your husband.

Kyle asked, "Would you at least wear the diamond necklace and earrings when we go out? I won't ask you to keep them, but they would just look beautiful with your dress."

Hesitantly, Grandma agreed. Lisa typed up a rental agreement on the necklace set.

All week, Kyle made Grandma feel like a queen. It seemed like the week had flown by when we realized it was Saturday morning. While Kyle was getting his hair cut, my hair stylist and makeup artist came to the house, so Grandma and I didn't have to go out.

While the hair stylist was doing Grandma's hair, my makeup artist started my makeup. Then, we switched. By the time we were all done, Kyle had made it back and was showering, getting himself ready for the evening.

I was the first one dressed. When I came out the room and looked at myself in the mirror, I looked stunning. I had on an elegant sleeveless, pewter Versace silk evening gown with silver sequins around the top, black five-inch, open-toed ankle-strap shoes, black accessories, and a black clutch purse that matched my shoes. You couldn't tell me nothing. Grandma used to say, "Look at her. You can't hit her in the butt with a red apple!"

As I walked into the living room, there was a knock at the door. I paused for a moment and yelled to Kyle, "Kyle, are you expecting someone?"

Not answering my question, Kyle said, "See who's at the door!"

I walked over to the door and asked, "Who is it?"

No one said anything. They just knocked again. I opened the door and I couldn't breathe. Whew! There he stood again in a black-on-black, tailored tuxedo. For about five seconds, I couldn't say a word. Finally, I breathed, gasping for air because Gavin looked so good. This was a total surprise. He looked me up and down and said, "You are gorgeous. May I be your escort for the night?"

This time, Gavin waited for me to invite him in. I smiled and said, "Yes; I could use an escort for the night."

Gavin stepped in, closed the door, grasped my hand, and kissed it ever so gently. He looked me in my eyes and placed a gentle kiss on my lips.

I thought, *If he keeps this up, I'm going to have me a real live situation right here because we will not make it out of here to the show tonight.*

Kyle came from his bedroom wearing his black tuxedo with a champagne bowtie and matching handkerchief. My brother looked so good coming around that corner. We all complimented each other on how good we looked. I thanked Kyle for the wonderful surprise, but the grand finale was yet to come. When Grandma came down those stairs, everything in the room stopped and all eyes were on her. Grandma was so beautiful, and she had tears in her eyes.

Kyle ran to get his camera. I got Grandma a Q-tip and said, "Grandma, don't cry. You don't want to mess up your makeup."

Grandma was beyond gorgeous, and her ears were lit with those beautiful diamond earrings from Kyle's store. Kyle took beautiful pictures of all of us. I had no idea these two had collaborated and pulled this night together, but I was grateful. I kissed my brother on his cheek, kissed Gavin on the lips, and said, "Thank you, you two. If I don't get a chance to tell you, I've already had a wonderful night."

Upon arriving at the restaurant, we received so many compliments. But undoubtedly, my grandmother was the most beautiful person in the place, and she felt like it. This was one of Kyle's favorite restaurants. The whole staff knew him. Some of the staff recognized me from visiting the restaurant with him. We laughed all through dinner. After dinner, we were off to The Opera House. The show was amazing. By the time the show was over, Grandma had tears rolling down her face again. Kyle had really touched my grandmother's heart.

Grandma looked at both of us and said, "Your mother would be so proud of the both of you. I am so proud that you are my grandchildren. Gavin, you know since you were a little boy, you've belonged to me, too. I'm proud of you, too." Grandma kissed Gavin on the cheek, and we all shared a moment.

As we were leaving The Opera House, I noticed that Gavin gave the valet clerk a ticket. I'm thought to myself: *We all rode together in the car service, so why is Gavin giving the valet clerk a ticket?* The valet pulled Gavin's car around at the same time as the car service pulled up. Gavin shook hands with Kyle, kissed Grandma on the cheek and said, "Good night." Then he told me, "You're coming with me."

These two had planned this night to a T. Grandma gave me a look. As I went to kiss her, Grandma said, "Take a picture of the sunrise. I would like to see what it looks like."

What did she mean by that? She knew what Gavin had planned. I stood there with a smirk on my face as I turned to look at Gavin. He shrugged his shoulders and looked away. I wasn't sure what Gavin had planned for the night, but I was going to enjoy it.

~ ❧ ~

Gavin and I drove down Jefferson Avenue, listening to the most romantic piano and saxophone mix. We talked about how great the show was and how amazing the night had been thus far. It was about midnight when Gavin turned onto the bridge that led across the Detroit River to Belle Isle Park. The park sat between Detroit and Windsor, Canada. It was beautiful during the day, but usually closed at 10 p.m. We crossed the bridge and there was a police officer at the entrance. He walked toward the car and Gavin got out. They had a brief conversation and Gavin shook his hand. I could see something is in his hand, but I couldn't see what it was. The police officer moved the barricade and let us through.

I was totally in the dark about what Gavin was up to. We were at Belle Isle at midnight. We drove around until we reached the beach side of the park. Gavin reached in the back seat, handed me some slippers, and said, "Put these on so your heels don't get caught in the sand."

"My heels? What about my Versace dress?"

"Don't worry about your dress. You won't be in it long. Wait here."

I thought, *Oh, my goodness. What is Gavin up to?*

He popped his trunk, grabbed a bag, opened my door, took my hand, and helped me out the car. He put a blindfold on me and told me to hold his hand and to trust him. I didn't ask one question. One thing was for sure, I trusted Gavin. I could tell we were getting closer to the water because I heard the waves from the water roaring in the night air. I could also smell the water. The night was such a beautiful sight. The temperature was perfect for a night at the beach.

When Gavin took the blindfold off, there was a pallet on the sand with candles lit all around the pallet. It was beautiful. Gavin sat me down on the pallet and we talked. We had a deep conversation about our feelings, why I left, the affair, the baby, and how we were going to move forward. Gavin leaned in and kissed me gently. I was turned on and I wanted more of this night.

Gavin said, "This is the perfect night."

As we sat watching the water, Gavin got on one knee, grabbed my hand and said, "I love you. I'm in love with you. And I will always be in love with you. I let you walk out of my life once. I don't want that to happen again. Obviously, you didn't like the last ring because you gave it back." Gavin pulled a different ring from his pocket. "Mya Johnson, again I ask you, Will you marry me?"

This ring was more beautiful than the first one and my eyes filled with tears. I thought to myself, *I've loved this man since tenth grade. I've shared my whole life with this man.* I opened my mouth and said, "Yes! Yes, Gavin. Yes, I will marry you! And I'll be the best wife you've ever had."

We chuckled and Gavin said, "You will be the *only* wife I'll ever have."

Gavin put the ring on my finger and kissed me on my lips. He turned me over, unzipped my dress, and slid it right off me. Our kisses on each other's body were so passionate. Gavin continued to undress me while he kissed me, until we were both lying naked on the beach. As I waited in anticipation, he gently lifted both my legs into air. When he penetrated my body, I gasped for air.

"Gavin..."

As a tear rolled down my face, I let out a moan of relief and passion. It felt like we were making love for the first time all over again. I now knew I was truly in love with Gavin.

Gavin and I made passionate love on the Belle Isle beach, among the waters whistling and the still sounds of the midnight air. Our bodies moved to a rhythm I would never forget. We both moaned as we moved to the best music I'd ever heard. As we made love on the beach, I felt like Gavin was already my husband. This man was my first love, and I couldn't wait to walk down that aisle and become Mrs. Washington.

Mama, I hope you're proud of me. Grandma, I will take that picture of that sunrise, I thought.

I was getting married, and yes, Gavin was making love to me while I was pregnant.

Chapter 14
Kyle ~ Three Weeks Later

"If salt is used to preserve, Lord, please use the salt from the tears rolling down my face to preserve me and my body."

Naomi and I both had appointments with my team of doctors. Naomi's results from her test were in and she had to go into the office to discuss the results and next steps. I promised Naomi I would be with her every step of the way. Since everything has been exposed, it seemed as if Naomi and I had grown closer.

She was my true best friend. She knew everything about me. Things didn't seem so hostile between us anymore. I'd let my guard down. We talked more and spent more time together. Kyle Jr. seemed so much happier. He always questioned why his mother and I weren't together, and I'd never given him the real answer. I always responded, "Grown-up stuff."

At my last appointment, my doctor had performed a series of tests. This alarmed me because I'd secretly watched as Ronald slowly withered away.

When Ronald told Grandma and Mya that he didn't have long to live, I couldn't help but think that I would soon be there. It had only been weeks, but Ronald's white blood count had dropped so low that there was no return for him. There was nothing else they could do for him. He was surely going to die soon. Ronald never took care of himself, and the virus turned from a virus to full-blown AIDS. On his last run to the hospital, his prognosis from the doctors was that he only had days left.

Depression came over me. I couldn't bear the thought of my son watching me, his father and his hero die slowly. The thought of my son growing up without me and leaving Naomi to raise our child on her own, weighed heavily on my mind. I wanted to totally forgive Ronald, but I was still struggling with the resentment I carried in my heart, knowing I may not be around to see my son grow up.

I hated being in the same room with Ronald. Every time he was rushed to the hospital, Mya went to check on him. She sat by his bedside and always told me that Ronald asked about me. I always gave her such an evil look, but she never stopped telling me. Ronald had very little family, so not many people visited him. I didn't fault Mya for sitting with him because he was her father. Just because I was struggling with forgiveness, I couldn't expect her to feel what I was feeling.

I was still trying to make peace with everything that had happened in my life. Part of me knew the only way I was going to be free was if I made peace with Ronald. In one of many conversations with my son, he told me that forgiveness is never for the person who did the wrong. Forgiveness is for you to be free and for you to move on. I chuckled as I remembered that quote. I thought to myself, *Tell that to a boy who was raped and now carries the HIV virus.* I'd asked God over and over, "How do I forgive this man?"

Some people say that God knows everything we feel. But I've never read in the Bible where it says God was raped and contracted a disease that was killing Him daily. So, I was struggling with my walk with God because I didn't understand how He looked down and watched this unfold, yet he did nothing to intervene. What curse had come down on my family that made God remove His hand? What curse allowed so many calamities to take place in a young boy's and a little girl's life? No one was there to prepare Mya or me for the many vicissitudes of life we faced. The things Mya and I went through would stick with us for the rest of our life. But I had to find a way to forgive Ronald and set myself free from the *spirits in my bedroom*.

When Naomi and I arrived at the doctor's office, we sat in the waiting room. There was weird silence between us.

The night before, Naomi had called me over and had me go into the prayer room with her. We went into prayer and Kyle Jr. joined us until it was his bedtime. I thought I knew everything about my son, but I didn't know that he could pray. Watching him gave me hope and made me want to believe in God like he does. But I didn't understand God. I guess I wasn't supposed to understand Him. When I looked at my son, the way he loves God and the way he prays, it made me want to believe again. But I couldn't.

I was lost in my thoughts when the office door opened. They called Naomi first. We looked at one another.

I told her, "I'm here. I'm not going anywhere."

She stood up and slowly walked through the doors with the nurse. When the door opened again, my name was called. My hands were sweaty, and I got a nervous feeling in my chest. I walked back with the nurse. She took my height, weight and temperature, and asked me the normal questions. She wrote something in the chart, then showed me to a room and said, "The doctor will be right in." I kept watching the time on my watch. A minute felt like an hour. It felt like I'd been waiting for days, but it had only been three minutes.

Finally, I heard someone grab the doorknob. It seemed like the door opened in slow motion. When the door finally opened, my doctor stood in the doorway. My doctor was always professionally dressed in gray slacks, a white button-down shirt with a blue and gray striped necktie, black shoes, and a long white lab coat over his clothes. My doctor had funny-looking sandy brown hair. Every time I saw him, I chuckled to myself because his hair always went in two different directions.

Normally, my doctor came in and talked to me by himself. But today, when he entered the room, there was a team of doctors behind him. I was totally intimidated. I had no idea what was coming next. I felt my eyes fill with tears, but I wasn't going to let them fall. I looked my primary doctor in the eye, and I was sure he noticed the fear that was undoubtedly present in my eyes. He extended his hand to me.

"Hello, Kyle."

My grip was normally firm. I was always certain to give a nice solid handshake. But today, my handshake conveyed my fear, anxiety and nervousness over what would come next. I part my lips with a lump in my throat and responded.

"Hello, Dr. Oppenheimer."

Dr. Oppenheimer noticed the distress on my face and immediately said, "Let me introduce everyone and their roles."

Dr. Oppenheimer went around the room and introduced the entire specialized team. He informed me that these were the specialists who had been working on my case and he assured me that they were the best in the business. There were two hematologist specialists, an HIV specialist, an AIDS research specialist, a specialist who only handled infectious diseases, and my doctor, who was also an HIV specialist. Together, they had 122 years of combined experience. After he introduced each specialist, he went around the room and allowed each doctor to explain their findings on my case. Because they were speaking in medical terms, I only understood about a third of what each doctor was to saying.

After they got past all the doctor gibberish, Dr. Oppenheimer said, "Kyle, we have a rare case here. When we first tested your blood, we saw traces of the HIV virus. Each specialist here has tested your blood over and over, and all eight of us have come to the same indisputable conclusion."

"Doc, you're making me nervous. Just give it to me straight."

"We can't find any more traces of the HIV virus or AIDS. Your white blood cells tested perfectly normal. You are free from this virus. When we drew your blood the last time you were here, I was the first to run it. When it came back clear of the virus, I called the team in to verify my findings. We all compared the samples of blood and everyone in this room came back on different days with the same conclusion: there is no virus. There isn't a trace, a trait or anything. You have a clean bill of health. I want you to discontinue all medication immediately."

I sat still for a moment. I couldn't believe what I was hearing. I couldn't move. After a long pause of silence, I said, "But, doctor, how could you see it, then not see it?"

"When we first ran your blood sample, your counts were down. Testing showed the virus was present in one test. But then, in another test, it was inconclusive. That's when I had to call in the different specialists because I have never seen this before. If it comes up in one test, it always comes back in the second one. So, I had each doctor here test your blood at their own facilities, and all of their tests are conclusive: no virus."

I didn't know what to say as tears rolled down my face.

"Kyle, you're one of the blessed ones." All the specialists wished me luck and exited. I was so emotional. When the doctors left the room, I looked up. I couldn't believe I was saying this. But I said, "Thank you, God." Before I left the room, I took a moment just to give God some praise.

As I exited the room, I saw Naomi waiting for me in the waiting room. I stopped at the desk and got my paperwork from the nurse. When I walked into the waiting area, Naomi looked at me, slowly stood up, walked toward me and said, "Let's go out in the hallway."

I was puzzled because she seemed so serious. I thought she was going to tell me that her test was positive. *How could that be? Mine was negative.* We stepped into the hallway and found a bench. As we sat down, Naomi asked in a cold voice, "So, what did the doctor say?"

I was totally alarmed and quickly became defensive. I responded, "Wait, Naomi. What did the doctor say?"

She turned and looked at the ground. "Naomi, what did the doctor say?" She looked at me with a smirk on her face.

"My test was negative. I don't have anything." I grabbed her and we hugged. I was so happy. I couldn't wait to tell her my news. Naomi looked at me. "Well, what did the doctor say?"

I told Naomi everything that happened when I went into the room. I told her about all the different specialists and how intimidated I was. Then, I told her what they all said. I thought we would have a praise fest right there in the hallway. Naomi jumped up and we both started dancing. I grabbed Naomi and locked her close in my arms. She looked me in the face. I pressed my lips on hers, and she pressed her lips back on mine. It had been a long time since I'd felt this close to Naomi. I almost forgot where we were. I pinned her against the wall, and we kissed like we were in a bedroom. After we kissed, we just looked at each other. I said, "Let's go home." I wasn't sure what that kiss was the start of, but I knew for sure it wasn't the last kiss.

We were getting ready to leave when I stopped. "Naomi, wait."

My doctor's office just so happened to be in the same hospital where Ronald was. I stood there, contemplating if I should go see him. Naomi knew just by the puzzled look on my face. She grabbed my hand and told me, "It's time."

We walked around to the information desk to find out what room he was in. We took the elevator up to that floor. I didn't know that he was in the hospice unit. There was also a *Do Not Resuscitate* (DNR) order on him. I stood outside his room, still hesitant and afraid to face my fears. But then, a sense of peace came over me. As I was getting ready to confront the man again who had ruined me as a child, Naomi was by my side. She encouraged me to go in the room and told me she would stay outside.

I finally went into the room. When I saw Ronald, he looked like he had aged thirty years. I barely recognized him. I sat in silence for a few moments as I read the numbers on the monitors. The breathing machine was doing most of the breathing for him; he could barely open his eyes. I watched him in silence. He was unable to speak because of the tube coming out his mouth. But he nodded his head to let me know he knew I was there.

All these years, all I'd ever wanted was for this man to die. I had wished death upon him so many times. I wanted to rejoice at his downfall. I wanted to feel happy because it appeared he was getting exactly what he deserved. But why wasn't I happy? Why did I still feel inadequate? I wanted to be happy, but I wasn't.

I used to pray Ronald would die a slow death. I never thought God was listening. I hoped him dying like this was not the result of my prayer because I was not rejoicing the way I thought I would be. I still felt hurt, but I felt different now that I was watching him die. I was standing in front of the man who destroyed everything that was supposed to be good in me. I was never supposed to make it through the abuse. I was supposed to die in my depression. I was supposed to live in bondage for the rest of my life until it killed me. But greater is He that's in me . . .

I was still struggling with hating this man, but a small part of me wanted this man to live. I wanted him to see my victory. I wanted him to see how I overcame the shame, the hurt, the embarrassment and all the resentment. I didn't know Ronald's story. I couldn't care less why, or even how, he became the monster he was. I could only imagine that the same thing must have happened to him in his childhood to make him become that person.

The difference between in him and me was that he didn't have a praying mother, a praying grandmother, a praying friend and a praying son. Most of all, he didn't have a calling on his life as I did. I had been called to get my life together and get right with God. I was called to be great. I was called to be a father to my son. I knew I was called to be a man of God with no more fear. No more self-hate. No more using women. I took control of my mind, and I would never let anything, or anyone, control my thoughts again.

I stood there, staring at Ronald. I could see him trying to look at me. As I released Ronald from my spirit, I found myself thinking of unplugging all the machines, one by one. But all I could do was pray for him.

"Father, in the name of Jesus, I pray for Ronald in his time of trouble. I pray you ease the pain he feels. Make his transition peaceful. I pray you throw his evil deeds in the sea of forgetfulness and I pray he knows you. I thank you for my deliverance. Lord, I exalt you as the highest name. Lord, I pray you forgive Ronald for the things he did knowingly and unknowingly, in Jesus' name."

Ronald's breathing became more and more faint. I sat and watched him gasp for air as I talked to him. I told Ronald how the things he did affected me. I also told Ronald that I was HIV-free. As I talked, I saw a tear roll from his eye. In this moment, I remembered my mother holding her chest, gasping for air—like Ronald was now gasping for air.

Then, I asked, "Do you confess your sins and acknowledge the things you did to me?"

He blinked his eyes slowly. I stood there, watching him trying to breathe. It seemed as if he was waiting for me in order to take his last breath. I grabbed Ronald's hand, looked him in his eyes, and said, "Ronald, I forgive you. You can rest in peace now."

In that moment, I knew that Ronald was waiting to see me before he made his transition. This was why he always asked Mya if I was coming to see him. Ronald closed his eyes and I felt a tear roll down my face. As I held his hand, Ronald took his last breath and the machine made a loud, long beep, which made the nurses and doctors come running into the room. I heard over the PA system, "We have a Code Blue!" As they rushed into the room, I stepped out. Naomi looked at me. I looked back at her and she knew it was over. Naomi put her arms around me as the nurses checked for a pulse. When they didn't find one, they pronounced Ronald dead. The nurse stepped out of the room and asked if I was family.

"Yes, he was my stepfather. I forgive him and now I'm free."

Chapter 15
Kyle

Since the age of twelve, all I'd ever wanted was for this man to die. Now that he was dead, I wasn't sure how I truly felt about it. I wasn't happy, but I wasn't sad either. For fourteen plus years, I'd held on to the anger and unforgiveness I had for Ronald. There I stood, viewing his body. Had this been a month ago, I wouldn't have been standing there.

Grandma and Mya made all the funeral arrangements. I didn't understand why we were having Ronald's funeral at the church when he didn't even belong to one. But my grandmother believed everyone should have a homegoing in a church. I believed if it was their choice not to go to church when they were living, then we shouldn't bring them into the church when they died. Maybe that was a little rough, but that was just me.

On the day of the funeral, Mya and I entered the church. I was surprised the pastor and some of the members of the church remembered us. Everyone was so much older, but they still had pictures of my mother, Mya and me on the wall in a memorial case. My mother and grandmother had been predominant figures in this church. My mother was the youth and choir director, head nurse and president of the pastor's aids. She meant so much to this church. I looked at the wall of memories and it brought a tear to my eye seeing Mya and me so young. I looked at my mother and how beautiful she was. I went into the basement and stood in the very spot my mother beat my behind for hitting Naomi on the butt. That was one whipping I was happy to get because it was my first time hitting a girl on their bottom.

When I went back upstairs, I saw Mya and Gavin looking at the same wall. Mya was crying as she looked at Mom's pictures. I let Gavin console her because I was already emotional. Naomi and Kyle Jr. accompanied me, and Gavin was there for Mya. Grandma had Granddad, so we all had someone there for each of us.

As I walked through the doors into the sanctuary of the church, the choir was singing. I felt a presence I'd never felt before. I was immediately overcome with emotion, especially when I saw Gavin's mother leading the choir, just like her and my mother did. People may have thought I was emotional because Ronald was dead. But my mind took me back to when we were happy with our mother and she brought us to this very church.

When it was my turn to view Ronald's body, I looked in the casket and remembered when the abuse from Ronald first started. I had flashbacks of the hurt and pain I'd suffered. I remembered the night my mother died, and I was stuck, staring at Ronald. I couldn't move away from the casket. I knew I had to throw all these emotions into this casket with him so I could free myself. I couldn't walk away from the casket with the same emotions I came into the church with.

My mother's face and Mya's smile flashed through my mind. Then, I felt my sister come up behind me. I was so relieved that I protected her. I wrapped my arms around her, and I finally got my moment of relief. Mrs. Washington stopped the choir and she started singing my mother's song. I was supposed to be there for the funeral, but my mind was on everything else. Even with all the people who occupied the room with me, I felt like I was in the room all by myself. It didn't matter anymore who saw me cry. All I knew was that I was crying.

The tables had turned. Now, my sister was there for me. She was holding me like I'd held her all these years. I couldn't believe I was allowing her to be there for me for the first time. It was almost as if she knew exactly what I was feeling. Mrs. Washington sang my mother's song directly to me. Finally, we were able to take our seats and it was time for the eulogy. The preacher stood at the podium and gave his Scriptures. He preached the sermon titled, "What I Went Through to Forgive My Enemy." It seemed like every word he spoke was for me. I sat and listened to his words, and it was as if God Himself was speaking to me. He said, "It's time to surrender your life unto the Lord."

I couldn't hold it anymore. I jumped up and yelled, "I want to give my life to Christ!"

The whole room got quiet. The preacher stopped preaching, and everyone started clapping. I looked over at my grandmother and she stood up with tears in her eyes. Grandma wrapped her arms around me and said, "It's time."

The pastor came from the pulpit. It didn't matter that this was out of the ordinary. He took my hand and presented me with the plan of salvation. I told that the preacher that I needed to be baptized because I didn't remember my baptism. Mya followed me and gave her life to Christ, as well. The church started shouting, singing and praising God. We forgot we were at a funeral. We started having church. I looked at Naomi and Grandma shouting, and I couldn't hold my peace. I let it all go and shouted throughout the church. I was feeling free—free from all the hurt, the pain, the agony, bitterness, lies, deceit, my whorish ways—free from everything that was done to me, and free from what I'd done to others.

I wanted to be baptized again so I could start a whole new life. I would be the man my son could look up to, admire and adore. I would be the husband that God saw fit for me to be. I truly understood what this journey meant for me now. I had no more shame. I would not mistreat another woman.

"Lord, I forgive Ronald, and I forgive myself."

I remembered my mother singing the song *Jesus Loves Me*. She'd taught this song to me when I was in the children's choir. However, I could now sing this song on my own with conviction. I understood what Jesus did for me. Ronald's life had a purpose and his purpose was to get Mya and me to this very point. Mya stood beside me and we changed our lives together. My sister and I were as close as close could get. We had shared the world together. Now, we shared God together.

The funeral proceeded and we laid Ronald to rest. What the devil meant for bad, God turned around for our good. Ronald's death brought me and my sisters' lives back to Christ. For that, I said, "Thank you, Ronald, and I truly forgive you."

Chapter 16
Mya and Kyle

KYLE ~

After the graveside service, Mya and I decided not to go back to the church for the repast. We barely knew Ronald's family anyway. Grandma, Grandpa, Gavin, Naomi, Kyle Jr. and The Washingtons all came back to my house. We had dinner and conversation. The Washingtons told Mya and me how proud they were of us. How we'd had to fight through so much and how we did it with such grace. I could never repay Mr. and Mrs. Washington for always being there for Mya and me. We all declared that, no matter what, we were a family. The next day, Mya and I went back to where our life started.

❦

MYA ~

When Kyle and I pulled up to our childhood park, I got so emotional. This was our safe zone. At this park, we could be honest about our life and our fears. We were able to speak about our situations for what they really were. We escaped the world in this park. We dreamed, played make-believe, and made life decisions here. This park was our world for many, many years. The pact Kyle and I made was that if we ever found ourselves separated from one another, all we had to do was make it to this park and the other one would be waiting.

We got out the car. At first, I just stood there and looked around. I grabbed Kyle's hand and we walked over to the very swing Kyle used to push me on. I sat down on the swing, and Kyle got behind me and pushed me. He didn't push me too high because I was pregnant. We reminisced and laughed like we did when we were kids. We left the swings and went to the picnic table, where we used to have all our deep talks. Kyle showed me our names which were still carved in the wood on the picnic table. I thought over the years they would have replaced the picnic tables, but they hadn't. It looked as if nothing had been replaced at the park. The grounds were well-kept over the years. But now, it seemed as if they weren't keeping them that well anymore.

We sat down at the picnic table and discussed what we thought our lives would be like now. I hoped Naomi and Kyle could reconcile their relationship because I didn't want another sister-in-law. I loved Naomi. She was always the best woman for Kyle.

Kyle and I discussed so much at the park. It was like old times. But the time had come for us to make the park our past. We knew this would be our last conversation at this park. We had a different direction now. I was getting married soon and my husband had to become my haven.

"Lord, I pray you'll make Naomi Kyle's safe haven."

I thank God that He spared my brother's life and gave both of us a chance to get it right. Listening to Kyle talk made me realize that I had been selfish. I always thought of myself, not paying attention that my brother was dying on the inside. My brother had always protected me, even before my mother died. To find out my brother had sacrificed himself so I didn't have to experience being molested or raped was something I could never repay him for. I couldn't hold back the tears, knowing what my brother did for me. With everything my brother and I had been through, we shared a bond that could never be broken. I will always love my brother to infinity and beyond.

Talking about Kyle's rape was the hardest conversation my brother and I ever had. I got a chance to see a different side of Kyle. I got to see the vulnerable side of him. Kyle was always strong raising me. I can't remember ever seeing Kyle cry. I held my brother and we cried, what I hoped was our last time. This park held all our innermost secrets. This park held our vulnerabilities. It was the only place Kyle and I could go to feel safe. Even after moving in with Gavin and his parents, this park was still our special place.

I can never repay Kyle for the sacrifices he made for me. All the nights Kyle had slept on my bedroom floor were for my protection. I will forever be indebted to my brother. I realized I had been a privileged little girl who was so self-centered, self-absorbed, egotistical and selfish. I had only wanted to see what I wanted to see, while my brother was fighting for his self-worth and self-assurance.

I thank God for my brother because, even though our home life was all messed up, Kyle made sure I dreamed. He made sure I stayed a kid as long as I could. I will forever be grateful for my brother. Many people say that a man leads his family to Christ. I'm saved today because I followed my brother to Christ. In my opinion, Kyle is a man with more strength and character than half the men alive. I thank God for my brother. He is my hero and I will forever love him. This is our story.

From the Writer

True forgiveness is one of the most important lessons to spiritual maturity. Thank you for reading *Spirits in My Bedroom*. This is a story loosely based on actual events. I am a survivor of rape and molestation, and I held a lot of unforgiveness in my heart. I had to learn how to forgive. I had to learn that *forgiveness* does not excuse what a person has done to you. True forgiveness sets you free from the bondage that unforgiveness holds you in.

I hope pieces of this story were enlightening to you. I hope this testimony teaches you. We all have challenges to face. There's a piece of me on each page. I have exposed portions of my life to strengthen you in yours. Thank you again, and remember, prayer is the key, but it's your faith that unlocks the door.

Now I lay me down to sleep.
I pray the Lord, my soul to keep.
I'm on my knees, just like you said.
God removed all the spirits from my bed.